The Chief Executive

Realities of Corporate Leadership

CBI Publishing Company, Inc.
51 Sleeper Street
Boston, Massachusetts 02210

THE CHIEF EXECUTIVE

Realities of Corporate Leadership
Chester Burger

Foreword by
John D. deButts

CBI

By the same author

Survival in the Executive Jungle (1964)

Executives Under Fire (1966)

Executive Etiquette (1969)

Walking the Executive Plank (1972)
(Also published as *Creative Firing*)

(*The Chief Executive* (1978) also
published in a special edition for The
Presidents Association)

Library of Congress Cataloging in Publication Data

Burger, Chester.
  The chief executive.

  1. Executives—United States. I. Title.
HF5500.3.U54B85   658.4'00973   77–2844
ISBN 0–8436–0747–5

Printed in the United States of America

Designed by Lauri Rosser

Printing *(last digit):* 9 8 7 6 5 4 3 2

To Jeff Burger

My son and my editor

Contents

Foreword

John D. deButts
Chairman and Chief Executive Officer
American Telephone & Telegraph Company

To observe that the responsibilities of the chief executive officer have enlarged dramatically in recent years is to state the obvious. Today more and more of the time that used to be spent in "running the business" must now be devoted to representing it to the many constituencies on which its future depends.

The activities of government have given a new dimension to the chief executive officer's job. Certainly they have to mine. Admittedly, AT&T is a regulated company. But—these days—what company isn't?

Day in and day out governmental policies are being made and administrative regulations are being promulgated that have a vital effect on the future of our business—in terms of the service we render to our customers and the security of the investment of our millions of owners. These regulations in many cases are being made not by elected officials who are accountable to their voter constituencies, but by the people within the Federal bureaucracy, by Congressional administrative assistants and the like. No doubt they believe their actions are taken in the public interest. But their accountability is far from clear.

We, however, are accountable—to our customers, to our owners, and to our employees. Therein lies the greatest challenge to the chief executive officer.

My fellow chief executive officers, who have discussed the problems of management in the chapters that follow, know that although the public may perceive business management as powerful, largely self-perpetuating, effectively answerable to no one and exercising a degree of power permitted to no other element in our society, the reality is different.

It makes very little difference that we who are presumed to be so powerful have very little occasion to feel that way. It makes very little difference that in real life the range of options open to management decision is—except at very high risk— much more restricted than the public imagines it to be. And it makes very little difference that for a very long time we have had a degree of government regulation over virtually every aspect of business operations as to leave very little question as to where the real power over the economy actually resides.

However, what counts in this regard is not so much power as it is the perception of power. So long as business management is perceived as exercising power unchecked by public surveillance or countervailing force, it risks further infringement on areas of private decision and—eventually—the deterioration of the incentives that makes enterprise enterprising.

It is therefore incumbent upon chief executive officers to demonstrate their accountability not only through right action but by their readiness to respond to every reasonable public inquiry about the policies and practices of their businesses. In the new environment we confront, it is essential that the CEO communicate constantly, both directly to the public and indirectly through the media. He should be accessible and responsive. He must *listen*. He must recognize that what we might have disposed to call "our" business is in fact the public's business, and that the public, hav-

ing a stake in our decisions, should have a voice in them as well.

The chief executive officer need not be the sole spokesman for his business. But there is no blinking the fact that he is the principal one. I count it as just about the first responsibility of my job to use every opportunity to respond to public concerns and to express those of our owners, customers and employees.

When the chief executive officer speaks, does anybody listen? In my experience the answer is yes. I recall an incident some time ago when a member of Congress advocated a position we regarded as detrimental to the interests of our customers and owners. I decided to seek a face-to-face meeting with him to express our viewpoint. When I flew down to Washington to keep my appointment, his administrative assistant was surprised, even shocked, that I came personally, and alone. He asked me, "Where are your men with the briefcases?"

None was with me. The Congressman was surprised as well that I had come alone, and he listened attentively to what I had to say.

Chief executive officers, it seems to me, should do this more often. We're not likely to get a hearing for our concerns unless we show ourselves sufficiently interested to voice them personally. It is for its readiness to do that that The Business Roundtable certainly has been effective. The CEOs who constitute its membership—and I am one—personally meet with public officials to present our viewpoints. We do not delegate this to our staffs, and I believe we receive a more attentive hearing as a consequence.

It is equally important that we meet the press, for there is no more important influence on the public's judgment of business—save for its direct experience of our products and services—than the impressions of our performance and our character that the public derives from the media.

Most businessmen are wary of the media, and I would be less than candid if I did not admit that from time to time, I have been also. But it is my conviction that only by our willingness to answer candidly and factually can we hope to banish such suspicions and superstitions as the public may harbor about us.

Within our own organizations, the day of the autocratic chief executive officer has passed. The management problems we face today are simply too complex to be decided by any one individual, however wise, however brilliant, however experienced. In our business, the ultimate responsibility and the ultimate accountability to the Board of Directors, who represent our owners, rests with me. However, my decisions aren't reached in a vacuum. In reaching them I have the benefit of the views of our Executive Policy Committee, which consists of myself, the President, two Vice Chairmen, three Executive Vice Presidents, and the Vice President and General Counsel.

The members of the EPC come to the meetings not as representatives of the departments they head, but as general corporate officers, jointly and severally responsible for the entire spectrum of our company's concerns. Our goal is to try to shape our own future, rather than simply let it happen to us.

We are assisted, of course, by specialists from the various departments and by our Corporate Planning Division.

But the specialists don't make our decisions. Top management must decide, as every chief executive officer knows all too well. The questions we face, even with the help of quantitative analysis, characteristically involve a high degree of uncertainty

and therefore of risk. When the experts have departed, we are left to ponder the imponderables, to weigh uncertain consequences against unforeseeable costs, to balance the interests of opposed constituencies, and finally, to decide. That is why the boards of directors have elected us.

The essence of the art of management lies in providing a direction, a purpose, and an order to the enterprise. At the same time, we must allow sufficient scope for those essential restless spirits who are constantly seeking better ways, whose management heresies may well become tomorrow's doctrine taught in graduate schools of business to the new generations of managers who will follow us. In selecting our principal associates, I derive one of my greatest personal satisfactions. Since the future progress of the organization for perhaps a generation to come will depend on the wisdom of our selections, it is understandable that we should take special satisfaction in seeing before our eyes the development of leadership equal to the challenges of today and the responsibilities of the days ahead that we cannot now foresee.

The chief executive officers who have discussed their experiences and problems so candidly with Mr. Burger have made, I believe, a real contribution to clarifying their role in today's society. Many have written about corporate management from the outside, but it is helpful to gain an insight into management problems directly from those who grapple with them daily. Certainly, they acquire a different perspective when one is sitting in the chair of the chief executive officer. For this reason, I commend Chester Burger for his contribution to an understanding of our new roles and responsibilities.

If a company has nothing going for it except one thing—good management—it will make the grade. If it has everything except good management, it will flop. That's the clear lesson of 50 action-packed years of U.S. business history.

In 1917, as in 1967, 100 great companies dominated U.S. industry. The startling fact, however, is that a clear majority of 1917's Top 100 are no longer members of that charmed circle today. Fifty-seven of the 100 have either gone out of existence or greatly declined in importance.

Behind all this turmoil and change is a mixture of galloping technology, social change, normal growth and decay. The academic community has poured forth a flood of books discussing these factors and their impact on business life. But all too many of the analyses have glossed over the most important single ingredient: the quality of top management. . . .

(Reprinted by permission of FORBES Magazine from the September 15, 1967 issue.)

Introduction

How our economy and our society function depends in significant part on how corporations function. And how corporations function depends in large measure on the performance of their chief executive officers. That's what this book is all about.

How do chief executive officers really function? What do they really do? How do they coordinate and direct vast numbers of employees, leading them in a common direction? How do they plan corporate strategy? Where do they draw the line between their responsibilities and those of the chief operating officers (who usually bear the title of president)?

What kind of men are they? Is it more accurate to characterize them generally as corporate autocrats or as "conductors of an orchestra," as one of them described his job to me?

These questions interested me, and preparing this book became my vehicle for seeking answers. Without doubt, many observers and social critics have been curious too. But not only social critics. Typically, after I had spent time with a chief executive, a senior official of his own company would phone me to ask, "What did he say?" Even these upper management people had not had the opportunity to hear the chairman express himself with candor and at length on matters affecting the future of the corporation.

In the executive suite, you do not hear talk of the current management theories and fads of the day. None of the CEO's with whom I talked ever referred to Theory X and Theory Y. That is not to say that such underlying concepts are unimportant.

But when you look at a large and complex enterprise from the perspective of the chairman,* neither problems nor solutions are so easily categorized. The chairman knows that Desired Result X will not automatically follow the application of Action Y; an inadequate president or vice president may intervene. (In one major corporation, the chairman, confronted by the Board with a president he did not want, simply put the man into an empty office and ignored him.)

But even if his chief operating officer is highly competent, a corporate chairman knows that uncontrollable and often unforeseeable factors may intercede to prevent attainment of his desired goal. Government regulations, usually originating at the Federal level, may suddenly eliminate an entire market, make production costs uneconomic, or make capital unobtainable.

Or public tastes may quickly and unpredictably change. Sometimes, these changes may be anticipated. But if such shifts appear obvious to the outsider after the fact, then why did General Motors and Ford Motor Company, demonstrably two of the best managed corporations in the world, look at the same set of facts, only to reach opposite and mutually-exclusive conclusions: General Motors judging that the public would demand smaller cars, Ford, the opposite? All those miles of computer output are useful, perhaps indispensable. But they cannot substitute for the judgment of a seasoned corporate management and, in the last analysis, its chief executive officer who must make the final decision.

*The word "chairperson" has not yet entered the vocabulary of corporate officers.

My own lifetime career has been largely involved in the management of the communications function. It would have been understandable, therefore, if I had devoted special attention to this subject in my conversations. I consciously avoided this temptation, because communications is only one of many problems facing the chief decision maker. Indeed, it seemed to me that chief executive officers often regard communications as primarily a problem of increasing the upward movement of information, rather than the dissemination of information downward through the organization and outward to the publics who are affected by the corporation.

The chief executive is preoccupied with learning what's actually going on through the corporate ranks. How can he know accurately how customers regard his company's products or services?

No shortage of information, computer printouts and reports exists for him. But what is significant? What statistic is more meaningful than all the other thousands of numbers? What numbers, not on the "bottom line," but buried in the operating data, should be looked into? Making such judgments emerges as a difficult aspect of the chief executive's post.

By contrast, the "downward" communications function receives less attention from many chairmen. It is more routinely handled and considered. I think this attitude is changing in the executive suite; there is more recognition that the CEO's strategic decisions will be neither understood nor implemented by middle management unless they understand them and accept them wholeheartedly. The same is true also of production workers; engineering aided by the computer has eliminated most of the repetitious, tedious jobs that required little thought and less understanding. With the widespread entry of the microprocessor into even routine production operations, armies of data processing specialists are assuming still greater importance. They need to know why things are done as they are; the best senior managements are finding innovative ways to tell them.

In the few months between the time these conversations took place and the time this book is published, changes will probably have occurred in the status of several of the CEO's included in this book, either by mortality or by action of the boards of directors. The chief executive officer does not hold a secure position. He is accountable for the success of the enterprise to his board of directors. They may replace him because of wrong decisions taken far down the line, about which he may have known nothing, but failed to act upon speedily when the problems became apparent. Or he may be, and frequently is, replaced because the times have changed. For instance, while he might have special expertise in marketing, now his corporation's major concerns may have become problems of relations with the government, where directors regard him as less effective. The job is no sinecure.

Nor is the chief executive officer, at the pinnacle of corporate power, a free agent, able to act arbitrarily as he chooses. Availability of financial resources, skilled manpower, public attitudes, government regulators, and the like circumscribe his freedom of action. Observing some of the nation's top corporate executives at work, I was impressed with their ability to reach sound decisions despite too little information, too little capital, and too little ability to forecast the future.

There is no dearth of information available about the corporate structure, corporate finances, or marketing activities of the companies discussed in this book. They are with one exception, public companies, and, again with that same exception (deliberately selected as counterpoint for that reason), among the largest corporations in America.

Business magazines report on them frequently and thoroughly. Most press reports are immediate and timely. The larger part of business reportage, however, is filtered through the perceptions and words of reporters, editors and academicians. My approach, instead, has been to allow the chief executives to discuss their roles in their own words, rather than mine. I have been interested not in the state of their corporations at a particular moment, but rather in how these corporate executives perceive and exercise their roles and responsibilities on a continuing basis.

Almost all the conversations took place in the "executive suite." Usually, they lasted for a couple of hours. Neither the CEOs nor I had notes to refer to, nor were they provided with my questions in advance. In each interview, I sought to concentrate on a particular area of management, so that the totality of management responsibilities would be discussed in one chapter or another, but not in each chapter. The indispensable tape recorder took it all down faithfully.

To assure accuracy, I submitted the edited text for each chief executive's approval. Interestingly enough, none altered his remarks significantly. Most added or subtracted only a few words here and there, usually for clarification and without bending the substance of the original remarks. The single major deletion was a frank discussion of a delicate internal corporate matter, where, said the Chairman, "My words aren't essential to the substance, but they would cause severe embarrassment to several people here." So out they went.

Other than that, the conversations are presented substantially as they took place. If some important area was omitted, the reader must blame not the chief executive but me for failing to ask the right questions.

Many of the chief executives who talked with me have rarely, if ever, previously discussed their management style and philosophies. In several cases, considerable efforts were required to secure their cooperation. The most persuasive argument I could muster was that the vast archives of published works on management contain relatively little written by those who actually hold the chief executive's post.

My special gratitude and appreciation goes to my son, Jeff Burger, who skillfully transformed the raw transcript of each conversation into the form in which you read it here. When I wrote my first book, *Survival in the Executive Jungle*, Jeff was a lad of fifteen. Understandably, a father takes special pride in seeing his son mature and develop into an able editor.

As the ideas for the book germinated, my wife, Elisabeth, made important and useful suggestions both as to the selections of CEOs to be included, and in the lines of questioning to be developed. My partner, Jerry A. Danzig, also assisted with helpful critiques on numerous occasions.

My executive secretary, Mrs. Carolyn Woods, and her assistant, Sharon Terry, shepherded the book from beginning to end, with unfailing efficiency. To them especially, and to all the others who assisted, I am deeply grateful.

Chester Burger

Chester Burger & Company, Inc.
New York City
October, 1977

William C. Norris

Chairman and Chief Executive Officer
Control Data Corporation

William C. Norris was a Nebraska farm boy who lost little time in becoming the epitome of the American entrepreneur. He entered the world of computers early, in the US Navy during World War II. After the war, he helped found Engineering Research Associates, which soon was merged into Sperry Rand Corporation. There, Bill Norris' creativity and driving leadership soon made him vice president and general manager of the Univac Division.

In 1957, he went on to found his own company, Control Data Corporation, which has grown rapidly to annual revenues of $2 billion, and assets of $5 billion. In 1972, he settled his antitrust suit against IBM for $101 million and IBM's subsidiary, Service Bureau Corporation, which made Control Data the world's leading company in electronic data services.

Control Data operations span Europe, the Middle East, Africa, Latin America and the Far East. The company is an innovator, a trail blazer, and Bill Norris is the man who put it all together.

Mr. Norris, you told me when we arranged this interview that you helped to found two small companies. Is that experience relevant to running a vast corporation like Control Data?

Well, I think it's relevant in many ways. Small business is really the root of our business society, and it's good to understand what's down there at the bottom. But also important is the flexibility, the creativity, the free communications of a small company. Some days, if you haven't had the experience of running a small firm, you wonder if those things are really possible.

They're easier to achieve in a small company?

Yes. When I helped to start Engineering Research Associates and later, Control Data, each was small and very innovative. Then they grew. Engineering Research merged with Sperry Rand. Control Data built up assets of $5 billion. And, in each case, the innovation and personal contact decreased. I'm not depreciating large companies like ours. They do a number of things—like product refinement, volume manufacturing and marketing—better than the small ones. But the little companies definitely have the edge in some areas.

Why do you believe that a little firm can innovate more effectively than a large one like yours?

Well, for one thing, they can afford to take much bigger risks. In speaking to people in small business, I often point out that all they've got to lose is their company. They look at me strangely, but I say, "You know, your company isn't very big and nobody will miss you if you fail."

Could you expand on that?

Sure. If someone has a small company, I guess that's the last thing he wants to lose. But if he really believes in innovation, he can make the commitment to bet his company on it. Whereas, because of the pressures of stockholders, management pride, the system and so forth, it's awfully hard in a big company to make a decision where so much is at stake.

Is the bureaucracy of a big company a major factor?

No question that it stifles innovation. It's a great mass going down one track. Take the young MBA's. They're almost the greatest killer of innovation there is. All they look at is the here-and-now. But you can't run a company with that mentality.

Take something like computer-based education. It took almost fourteen years for us to get it to the marketplace. There were many times, in fact, when someone would say about me, "Well, Christ, he's been at it for fourteen years. What makes him think it's going to go now?" And that's your MBA mentality. And if you have a guy who wants to go off in another direction, it's just impossible; he'll get swept along with the management. Maybe people don't even think his idea is bad. But it's a matter of priorities. Also, most people have a tendency to think that that which is like what they know is good, as opposed to that which is radically different. That's another problem for the man with an innovative idea. People are afraid of it.

Can you give me an example?
Mass memory, a project related to our computer-based education program. One of our project engineers was strongly behind it, but another approach emerged. And the man who supported that one had more control over funds, so the momentum went to him. When we hit hard times and couldn't afford both systems, mass memory got killed. But I felt there was important technology there, and about that time we settled the IBM law suit. So, I told my people, "Dammit, we got all this money to help us make up for the past, so you can have some of that to develop this technology. Well, good thing we did. Because now we're using that technology to solve some problems in the other approach.

This was a case of innovation that survived despite the system.
Right, but only because I personally made sure that it got the funding. I don't think anyone else could have saved it.

In the early days of Control Data, was risk-taking more prevalent?
Oh, yes. We actually bet the company three times. And we damn near lost it.

What happened?
Well, the first time was with the 1604, our first large-scale computer. We had enough money to carry it to where we could demonstrate credibility, but not enough money to complete it. At the last moment, we got a government contract, finished the project and had a big success.

If you hadn't you would have gone out of business?
Oh, we'd have been broke. No question about it.

You were already a public company then, and still you took a risk?
Yes, sir. However, I think I had a little advantage. When we sold stock, much of it to people I knew, I pointed out the risk involved. And I'm the biggest stockholder. I told them, "If the company goes broke, I'm going to be worrying about my loss, not yours. So don't come hollering to me if we lose." Which, as I said, we didn't.

Tell me another instance.
During 1965, on our 6000 series computer, we ran into much more severe technical problems than we'd anticipated and IBM hit us hard. We almost lost. We went almost a year without being able to get an order. That was a rough squeeze. Then in 1970, about eighteen months after we had acquired Commercial Credit Corporation, we had serious problems. Sales started going down due to the recession. At the same time, we had seven large development projects under way. One of them was computer-based education. Others included the development of data services, the development of two large computers, mass file memory. These were all central to the long-range success of the company. I didn't want to just have a company. What was interesting to me, and I thought important, was to have a company that was going to be here permanently. Therefore, I was not willing to compromise to make the short-term safe. As a consequence, we had a hell of a lot of problems and almost lost our commercial paper rating and Commercial Credit. The banks were on our neck. If we had concentrated on the immediate problems, it could have cut the guts out of the company. If we had cut out these programs, we could have made some profit in the short-term. But we'd have sacrificed forever the long-term opportunity.

You couldn't bring yourself to do it?
No, I couldn't. I thought about it a great deal. It wasn't my money and I didn't want to get my own personal objectives mixed up with the stockholders' money. But I was looking to the future. I think that it's important to build a permanent organization with the good jobs. As a consequence of having taken those risks, we're providing a hell of a lot more jobs today than we would otherwise. We'd have just been a runt today.

Now that you're too large to take risks like that very often, you've set up joint ventures between Control Data and a number of small companies.

Yes. We've been at it since 1962. We realized then that the technology required to be most effective in the computer systems business had simply become too broad for us—or any other single company—to cover. So we began working out cooperative programs. And today, we're involved in joint ventures in virtually every area of technology important to our business. In most cases, we've hooked up with small companies, because I think those arrangements give each party the best of both worlds.

Give me an example of one of these cooperative ventures.

Sure. We need an electronic beam memory for our computer-based education program. And Microbit—a small company with just a few outstanding people—had an idea. They came to us and needed financing for the project. We felt it would be desirable to share the risk on this and to get others involved. And we did. Well, the others have fallen by the wayside, but new backers have been found. We now own 46 percent of the company.

You didn't try to acquire them outright?

No. If we had, they would have run into problems. I want them to be living on a shoestring, because they'll try harder that way. You can't innovate to the maximum degree unless you've got enormous incentive. You have to be almost drowning to really do your best.

And Microbit is proving the truth of that philosophy?

Yes. They're coming up with a great, great product.

How do they like the arrangement?

Well, they like it. It's the only way they could possibly survive.

What's their management style? Are they informal, less casual, less organized?

Too casual.

By your standards.

Sure. But now isn't the time to take issue with that. Wait till they get the product. And we try to introduce as much discipline into the organization as we can. And it works. They have a great dedication, a burning desire to succeed with this project. They said they could do it, and by God, they were right.

You're interested in developing this sort of joint venture with companies and countries throughout the world.
Absolutely. We're doing it. We believe that all countries and relevant companies within them should be working actively to develop cooperative scientific and technological programs. Even though the United States is the world's most technologically advanced nation, we just don't have the resources to solve all our problems on our own. You know, I'm talking about energy needs, health care, the environment, education. With cooperation from other countries, we could solve these problems a lot sooner.

Control Data's cooperative ventures extend to the communist world.
Yes, we have a much more active and comprehensive effort in those countries than any other US company. For example, we have a wide-ranging ten-year pact with the Soviet Union. We have a joint project going on in Poland. And we have a factory in Romania, owned by us and that government, to manufacture printers, tape units and card equipment. We've been told by the Russians, incidentally, that we've seen more of their plants and technology than all other American firms combined. That should give you some idea of the scope of our exchange program.

Could you explain the philosophy behind it?
First of all, a third of the world is communist and there's a message there. They're out there whether you like it or not, and you have to reckon with them. God knows, I wouldn't want to be part of their system, but it has some attributes.

For example?
It puts a great premium on intellectual achievement. And, as a consequence, those people are generating more new information than we are here in the US. The way for a young person to get stature, money, and everything else in Russia is to get an advanced degree in science, so that's what they work toward. Their system continues to emphasize intellectual achievement. You know, they've got a smaller Gross National Product than we do, but over the past ten years, their scientific and technical establishment has consistently been 20 percent larger than ours. So, in hardware, they have the latest technology.

What don't they have?

They're vertically integrated. They don't have hundreds of little companies for different specialties. And there's very little communications among industries. Hell, an industry is just like a foreign country in Russia, one to the other. Also, they don't have any marketing organization, so they have no way of knowing what the world wants. They're all bound up in their system. And they talk about innovation; hell, they can't innovate for nothing when it comes to products, because they don't have the marketing perspective. So, we have a great opportunity to do business with them. In the simplest terms, our system emphasizes product innovation whereas theirs creates information. And we're running out of information.

What about ideology? Do you ever have misgivings about working with the communists?

Well, they need us and we need them. I think ideology has no place in business. Also, I've often said that we don't really have anything to fear from the communists. As long as we remain strong and productive and have a powerful military, we'll be okay.

Yet the government is critical of your dealings with the Soviets.

Yes, particularly the Department of Defense. Their philosophy is to sell them as little as possible and to make it difficult for companies who are in the high-technology area to do business with them. They deny that, but that's really what they do.

Can I quote you on that?

Absolutely. I had a meeting with then Secretary of the Treasury Simon who, I was told, was more business-oriented than anyone else in the cabinet. I told him that we're having problems with several large orders because the Department of Defense's administration of export controls is in the hands of biased, poorly-informed nonexecutives.

How did he react?

He took it personally and he got angry. I said I wasn't talking about him and he said, "Yes, you are, because I'm involved in the review of every one of these cases you mentioned." I said, "Well, I have yet, Mr. Simon, to run into one person in the Treasury, Commerce or State Departments who has both enough expertise in computer technology and enough guts to stand up to the Department of Defense."

What did he say then?

That I obviously hadn't met his staff. And I said that I sure would like to get acquainted with them, but that I thought he was getting biased information nevertheless. Then he said that, in any event, the National Bureau of Standards would be reviewing the cases and that they're not biased; they're really scientists and aren't connected with the military. But I explained to him that the Bureau didn't have the funding for the job, which he apparently hadn't known. So he said, "They're going to get funded. If the Department of Commerce won't do it, I will." And to that extent, I was very pleased with the meeting. But the problem with the Department of Defense remains. On virtually every project with the Soviets, their starting point is that we're not going to do it. And that's not what I'd call fair administration.

They believe that if we help the Soviets with modern computer equipment, we'll increase their efficiency and enhance their war-making potential. Do you see any truth in that at all?

Well, the sale of any data processing system will advance the productive efficiency of the customer. But on the level we're speaking, it's a matter of degree. You know, food is more fundamental than anything we've got in data control, because a guy can't fight if he can't eat. And we sell them food. The government wants to sell them more.

Where do you draw the line?

As far as I'm concerned, unless technology is very new and fundamental, forget export control. You know, the Russians aren't suffering from lack of military capability. They've got it, God knows. As for the areas we're dealing in, if we don't sell to them, somebody else will. Or they'll develop the technology themselves. They're doing it.

How can you be sure?

We've seen what they've already got. Their RYAD 1040 is comparable to medium-sized US computers. It eliminates the Eastern European market for that kind of equipment. And the more powerful RYAD 1050; that's being developed and built in the Soviet Union. It will probably eliminate Eastern European markets for the larger US computers. All that we'll be able to export to them are some peripheral equipment and certain large special-application computers.

Have they got the capability to build them as well?

Yes. Their technology has advanced to a point where they can meet any computer need with their own resources. It's just a matter of priorities as to whether they purchase or build themselves.

Is the US Government really aware of this?

No. You know, we brought a RYAD 1040 to Washington and the US military people were just amazed at the level of development. They could hardly believe it was real. I told them, "Kick the tires. It really works." I think their misconceptions about the level of technology in Socialist countries are hindering export of our computer equipment to the Soviet block. The Pentagon is also limiting business opportunities for licensing, co-production and technology exchange.

Did your RYAD display affect the government's attitude?

Not really. They said, "Well, if we can just delay them for six months, it's worth something to us." But the Department of Defense's greatest asset is the industrial base of the US. And jobs are becoming a precious commodity here. If a hundred jobs are involved in an export matter, I think it should have the highest level of consideration.

How many Control Data jobs depend on export or foreign trade?
A third. About 10,000 jobs.

Besides increased employment, what do you consider to be the prime benefit of your trade with Russia and the other socialist countries?

As I said earlier, we're gaining information. We have joint projects going on with Russia in nuclear fusion, for example, where some of their efforts are just outstanding. There's another area, magnetohydrodynamics, where they've done some very important work. That means power generation. Now, this is work that has gone up to the applied stage, and, of course, in the theoretical stage, there's a lot of work in mathematics, physics, chemistry.

You're impressed?
Oh yes, hell, it's there!

As one of the most advanced technology companies in the United States, aren't you in a very strong position to sell abroad?

Yes, and, of course, it's in the high technology area where we have the balance in our favor. We need to have some relaxation of export controls before this will be significant to us, but we'll get there eventually.

What are some of the roadblocks?
The so-called Jackson Amendment which made it possible for the Department of Defense to veto any particular export case. The President can override it. But if he overrides it, he must take it to Congress and I don't think the President will do that for any one case.

Jackson's policy was to make trade with the Soviets more difficult?
Oh, yes. It was a political drive to get support from some of the Jewish community by pressing the Soviets to allow more Jews to emigrate. Well, we lost the trade, and the Soviets seem to be allowing fewer Jews to emigrate. So it didn't work.

Meanwhile, have you lost business as a result of other US export policies?
Absolutely. In one recent case, a French firm obtained a $75 million contract to build a multi-layered printed circuit board plant in Russia. The opportunity had been discussed previously with Control Data, but the US government discouraged us from pursuing it. I could give you a number of other examples.

What do other business people think of all this? Are they interested in trade with the communists?
Well, I think things are changing now. In just the last year, for instance, General Motors has been very active over there in trying to set up plants and joint ventures. But I think that, in general, there's still a reluctance to accept the fact that we can get valuable knowledge from the Russians. People think we can do everything better than everyone else. That just isn't true anymore. There's a national arrogance, and I think it's pitiful.

If you had your say, what would our national policy be?
Well, we need a better defined, more aggressive trade program with the socialist countries. And I think, first of all, that we should develop better methods of collecting and disseminating information on the status of their technology and on the business opportunities they present to us. I think also that the present adversary relationship between the US gov-

ernment and business should be changed to a partnership. And finally, I believe that we should set up a technology exchange program—at a level of at least $25 billion over five years—with the Soviet Union.

With those views, the Soviets must see you as a sort of oddity among American capitalists.

To an extent, yes. I understand their excellence in science and I understand the merits of doing business with them.

So they like you?
Oh, yes. I made the front page of Pravda.

Have any of their high officials sat down and talked with you on a personal basis?
Sure. For example, when we set up our plant in Romania, which was a major joint venture, I found out that the guy I was dealing with liked to fish, and we did some of that. My wife was with me and I think one of the nicest experiences we've ever had was that fishing trip on the Danube.

What is the old saying, if you go fishing with someone . . ?
Well, I've never known a no-good s.o.b. who liked to fish. It really gave me a helpful insight into the man, because we've since been able to work through some hellish problems and the joint project is going to be very successful. I'm glad of that, partly because this is the sort of venture that I think can help improve relations between our country and the socialist block.

In other words, then, you're concerned ultimately with more than just profits.
Well, profit is certainly at the core of our economic system. And, of course, we want to make money. But there's more to business than profits. It's important to remember that no corporation has a God-given charter. We exist at the will of society; and we'll lose our charter if society decides we're not sufficiently responsive to its needs.

Your response to America's internal needs seems as unusual as your efforts abroad. For instance, you don't believe in corporate contributions.
No, not really. Control Data does make them, but the amounts are peanuts. I've been on the boards of large companies. I've seen the process of making corporate contributions. I've also seen what happens. No matter

how large the contributions, there's a feeling on the part of the average guy out in the community, "Why didn't they do more?" You can't win that game. Of course, there's the United Way, and other agencies. They are very necessary, but I believe that supporting them is a responsibility, not of just big companies, but of everybody, individually.

Why?

We take the position that the larger part of cash contributions should be met by individuals and that business should address itself to the societal needs that individuals can't meet, like providing jobs and better housing, improving the quality of education and health care. That sort of thing.

But Control Data does encourage charitable organizations to solicit employee contributions.

Oh, sure. I believe in that. And I contribute myself—as an individual. But as a corporation, I think we must find ways to turn the needs of society into business opportunities. That's what our capitalist system is all about.

So you undertake projects for the good of society, but you make sure that they have sound business objectives as well.

Exactly. You know, people don't want charity. They want jobs and an environment where they're free to choose their own directions.

What have you accomplished toward that end?

I could give you a number of examples. Back in 1968, black residents of inner cities faced an especially great need for jobs. At the same time, we needed to increase our production. To address both these needs at once, we built new manufacturing plants in inner-city communities in Minneapolis, St. Paul, and Washington, DC. We expected the plants eventually to show a profit for us, of course. But, equally important, they meant jobs for the residents of those communities. We went out of our way to make a substantial investment to hire blacks, to train them, and help them to become as productive as any other class. We've done that, and it has cost money, a lot of money. But that is the sort of thing I'm talking about. And that's expensive.

You imply it wasn't easy.

Hell, no. Most of these people had never had a regular job before. They weren't accustomed to the routine of working regular hours. They had hellish problems. Problems with family and children. Sometimes alcohol or drugs. You couldn't just hire them and let it go at that. We had to provide a very special type of personnel setup to help them. Legal help. All kinds of help to keep them on the job. We didn't want to fire a man with problems. That would negate the objective we were trying to reach. So our people went to great efforts to salvage them.

How did you get your first-line supervisors to be attuned to really try to help, to carry out your objectives?

Well, sometimes we didn't. It was trial and error. In one instance, our main problem was the supervisor. In fact, in the beginning, we didn't have any blacks who were competent to run the plant. And so we picked a person we thought had empathy for the problem, and as it turned out, he hated their guts. It took us six months to discover that. During that period of time we didn't really make much progress. Eventually we found people who were sincerely sympathetic to what we were trying to do. And we succeeded.

What else are you doing to raise the number of minority group workers in your ranks?

We're aggressively recruiting at colleges attended primarily by minorities, for one thing. And we've established numerical goals and timetables for minority hiring. As a result, the percentage of minority employees involved in our US computer operations rose from four percent in 1968 to more than 10 percent in 1974. We've had to spend substantial extra money on training, but this is the sort of contribution that I strongly feel business should be making. It's money well spent.

Harry K. Wells

Chairman and President
McCormick & Co., Inc.

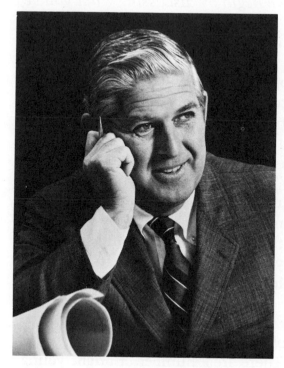

McCormick & Co., Inc., a specialty food company, manufactures and sells seasoning and flavoring products for home use through supermarkets, and to other food processors for use in their manufactured products. It also sells to the institutional market through food-service distributors.

A tiny, door-to-door operation at the time of its 1889 founding, the firm now gathers raw materials from thirty-five countries, operates twenty-seven manufacturing facilities and distributes its products in eighty-four countries. It employs nearly 5,000 persons to produce nearly a third of a billion dollars in annual sales. Harry K. Wells, who came to McCormick in 1946, has served as its president since 1969.

Mr. Wells is a native of Baltimore, as is his wife. For many years he has played a leading role in his city's cultural and economic life. A graduate of the University of Maryland, he is currently Chairman of the Maryland Council for Higher Education. He is a director of leading Maryland Corporations, including Maryland National Bank, Maryland Casualty Company and Baltimore Gas and Electric Company.

In industrial circles, Mr. Wells' leadership has been recognized by the directorships in the Grocery Manufacturers of America and the National Association of Manufacturers.

McCormick & Co. has earned a reputation as a pioneer in participative management—getting your middle management people, and even rank-and-file employees into decision-making. And we've heard repeatedly it's been successful. Could we begin by discussing what you've actually done?

Well, Multiple Management was introduced at this company in 1932. My predecessor, Charlie McCormick, came up with the idea. He felt that the best thoughts of a number of people could provide more effective leadership than the dictates of a few top executives. As a result, the company established first one and then a series of what we called "junior boards of directors." They consisted of supervisors and middle managers of our various units. The boards, which we now call Multiple Management boards, have been with us ever since. That's more than forty years. So it's nothing new with us. What we're doing is applying a democratic method of government to a business situation.

Charlie McCormick used to say that a businessman fulfills his function of profit-making best if he always remembers his obligations to his employees, his consumers and suppliers, as well as to the stockholders. That's all we're doing.

In practice, how well does it work?

In my opinion, extremely well. There are a number of bright young people on these boards, a lot of people who have ideas they want to get out and have tested. This is a vehicle that allows that to happen. We've gotten some terrific recommendations, too. For instance, that we ought to get into that product; we ought to get into this market; we ought to change that package; we ought to have a new kind of benefit. Many of these ideas have been quite good, quite profitable. But the boards' value extends way beyond these sorts of specific suggestions.

In what way?

For one thing, they help to broaden their members' experience. A board might include people with backgrounds in accounting, data processing and quality control, plus those in chemistry, sales and so forth. And when you start working on a project, each person will tackle what he knows, but there will be a lot of interaction. A salesman, for example, may be on a committee with somebody who has know-how in production. Let's say they're working on a plant problem. Maybe the salesman can't contribute directly to solving that problem, and maybe the plant guy can't do much on the marketing study that the project requires. But by working together, they gain a lot of respect for each other's skills. And by being exposed to each other, they both pick up a lot of knowledge.

It's a learning situation.

Right. Through the Multiple Management system, they have the opportunity to find out a great deal about our business. They interact with people of different backgrounds, people from different areas of the company whom they wouldn't otherwise have a chance to really communicate with.

Since you've been president, have you encountered any problems with Multiple Management?

Well, the whole mechanism is designed so that there's a turnover on the boards; people come on and go off. We've said to the members, and we mean it sincerely, that their participation won't have an impact on their regular jobs; this is extracurricular. The people who come off the boards are still sometimes hurt. There's no doubt about that. But overall, I think the system has an extremely positive effect in terms of general communication. You know, people talk to people in our company. When there are problems, we're not afraid to deal with them. People don't try to cover up so the boss won't know.

Do you find that your employees are generally candid even with you, the president of the company?

To a very large extent. I'm reminded of something that happened shortly after I took the job. A committee from one of the Multiple Management boards came to see me. And they made their point very delicately, but the message came through loud and clear that they were very disenchanted with a decision I'd made on one of their recommendations. They felt I'd aborted the system.

How did you react?

I said, "If I'm wrong, raise hell with me, but why am I wrong?" It turned out that after one of their recommendations had been approved, I'd changed a minor point without going back to them. I hadn't thought it was that important, but they took a different view. Anyway, we got it straightened out.

How? Through communication or a change in your decision?

Both. Our communication changed my decision. And I said that, in the future, since they all felt that strongly, I'd come back to them when we agree to carry something out to the letter and find we can't do it. The point is, here was a group of young fellows, members of a junior board, who were willing to take on the president because they thought I hadn't done what I'd agreed to do. Because of an underlying attitude that the company has developed over the years about how people interact, we have an atmosphere that allows anyone here to sit down and have meaningful dialogues about our policies and our objectives for the future.

Who appoints the members of these boards?

Mostly, they're not appointed at all. The boards select their own members by holding elections. The exceptions are those members of the sales board who come from the main office; they're appointed by the senior board. As for the senior board, its members are elected by the stockholders; and with very few exceptions, the senior board—the board of directors—consists of people who formerly served on one of the Multiple Management boards.

How does your election process work?

We've geared it to emphasize ability, not popularity. The members of the board rate each other on their performance. If I serve on a board, for example, I rate all the other fourteen members; they all rate me. The ratings are done every six months. The ratings are computed mathematically and the highest six constitute the membership committee that reforms the board and elects the people who will serve over the next half year. It's a continuing process.

And leaders emerge?

Right. The people who are continually successful on these boards, who are contributing ideas that their peers consider worthwhile, rise to the top. They're on the membership committee year after year, term after term. They're the leaders, the ones that have it. And it's not what the boss thinks of them; it's not what the president of the company thinks of them. They're being singled out by their own colleagues.

You give a lot of weight to this?

Absolutely. You know, we'd rather promote from within than hire people away from other firms. And the Multiple Management boards have proven to be an excellent training ground for our future leaders. We've had a high degree of success when people who shine consistently on the boards move up in management, because they have a track record of good performance. And conversely, if you find a person who has not fared well on a board, you can be almost certain that, in management assignment, he is going to encounter difficulties.

How much power can the junior boards exercise? I'm wondering, Harry, whether, in the lower echelons, board membership might be little more than an honorary thing.

Not at all. You know, we're not playing a game to make people feel important. They *are* important. It's true that suggestions of the subordinate boards must be unanimously approved by the board of directors before we implement them. But those suggestions only come to the senior board after they've received the approval of the lower board.

This protects us against the violent splits of opinion that sometimes develop on the boards. Sometimes somebody might come up with a wild idea, but he'll probably be unable to get full support. So when an idea is approved and sent up to us, the board of directors, we take it very seriously. And the vast majority of them are okayed.

So the members know it's worth their best effort?

Yes. Each member receives extra pay for the time he spends on board business. He knows that he has a job to do and responsibilities to fill. He knows that his fellow board members respect him, that his ideas can get a fair shake. If all this wasn't clear, the system simply couldn't work. We need it to work to help reach our objectives.

Let's talk a little about those objectives. You set very specific goals for the company. You have an annual sales growth objective of 12 percent, for example, and a 16 percent objective for growth in net income. How close do you usually come to meeting those marks?

Reasonably close, I think. We generally find that we exceed them in one time period and fall a little behind in another, because our business tends to be seasonal. So we look at our success not monthly or quarterly, but as a year-by-year kind of thing. You know, if you don't meet your sales objectives this year, you try to surpass them next year. A good long-term average is what we're really looking to achieve.

How do you set your objectives? For instance, last year, you had a goal of a 12.5 percent return on average assets employed. Why that instead of, say, 12 percent or 13 percent?

Well, it's a group decision. We look at what other businesses are doing and what our history has been and try to set objectives that seem to be in tune with both. We look at where the world would expect us to be as a progressive company and at what we're able to achieve and we come to a consensus. On the goal you cited, by the way, we're a little short now; we're closer to 11 percent. Our possible new investments, therefore, are viewed as having to be a good deal better than 12.5 percent in order to pull that average up.

Okay. Now, where down the line in your management do these goals begin to be formulated? Do you sit down with your managers at the beginning of the year or does it come from the bottom up or what?

It really works both ways. The head financial people at corporate headquarters do sit down to establish objectives for the various facets of business. Meanwhile, the operating people in the various operating units try to put together their objectives. And then we iron out the differences.

How far in advance do you plan?

It's an ongoing thing. When we're finalizing annual budgets and detailing plans for the next twelve months, we talk about short-term objectives. Then, at another time in the year, we have what we call "business reviews," at which five-year planning is discussed. So there are those two specific times; and a good deal goes on in between.

Now suppose I'm a plant manager and I go to a division manager with a suggestion about modernizing the production line at such and such a cost. What happens then?

Within the division, they would determine the necessary investment; we have certain criteria for doing that. Then, in the kind of case you mention, the information would be forwarded to the corporate manufacturing head. And he'd negotiate with the division manager: "Have you considered this factor? Are you sure that this estimate or assumption is correct?" That sort of thing.

Who would worry about return on the investment? The plant manager or the division manager?

Both. Obviously, the division manager would have a higher awareness of this. But all our plant managers, all the people who recommend investments, are becoming knowledgeable of the need to have a satisfactory return on the asset.

What makes you unusual is not just that you set very exact objectives and use input from the Multiple Management boards, but that you print your goals in black and white in your annual report.

Right. And for the past two or three years, we've been telling the security analysts about them.

Isn't that rather rare?

I think it's becoming more prevalent. We just thought, if we know what our objectives are, why can't we tell somebody else?

Maybe for fear that you'd get egg on your face if you didn't meet them.

Well, it doesn't really worry me that much. We don't worry about being unable to hold onto the stockholders. Our objectives are just that: places for us to aspire to, places we believe we can reach. When we don't get there, there's a reason. For example, while we did well in many areas last year toward achieving a 12.5 percent return on average assets employed, an onion and garlic crop problem hurt one of our subsidiaries and kept us from reaching the goal.

What did the analysts say?

Nothing very negative. I think there's a positive value in letting them see our goals. That gain more than offsets any problems when sometimes we come up short.

Still, don't they ever say, "Hey, what happened here? You didn't make your mark again."

We haven't had that reaction yet, to my knowledge. Though I'm sure the treasurer gets a few in that vein. But again, we see the objectives as something to go after, like putting a carrot out there to give you something to chase. If you continually exceed your objectives, they have no credibility.

By the same token, if your objectives are unachievably high, your people will be turned off.

That's right. You've got to put the carrot out far enough so it's a challenge to attain and not so far that it's impossible to catch.

And the security analysts realize this? They've been understanding?

Well, I think we get some good analysts who understand our business and our objectives. They're flexible enough to know that if we don't meet a specific goal, our overall growth won't be affected. You know, the best analysts are aware that there can be temporary setbacks, things over which we have no control. But we do get other analysts who really don't know the business. All they're looking at is numbers; they have no feel for our purposes, for where we're headed. They want you to eliminate anything that doesn't maximize your current earnings. They show little or no perception of the investment spending that we do to build new segments of our business, or even entirely new businesses. Sometimes, we have problems with this type.

For example?

We had one young man in here, a very bright guy, who kept pushing for more detail on the business. Questions like, "How much spice business do you have? What's your gross margin on spices? How much extract business?"

He wanted competitive information.

Right. We don't have those facts about our principal competitors. Why should we ourselves give them out? Anyway, this particular analyst kept probing for more details and I finally got mad. I said, "Damn it, you give me a pain. You want to know more about our business than you're entitled to know and more than you need to know."

Why do you think he was asking those questions?

I think what he really wanted to do was give me advice on how we should run the business. And I told him, "Look, if we'd sat down twenty-five years ago and I'd divulged all these things you're asking for, you would have said we ought to get out of the spice business and concentrate on other areas. Today you tell us we really ought to be in spices and we should get out of some of the other things that you don't think are lucrative." He wasn't looking at the long-term picture. I told him so.

How did he react?

He was very nice about it. He backed off finally and smiled and said, "My job is to ask the questions to try to maximize our investment. You're the one who has to decide to give up short-term results in favor of the long-term gain." I said, "That's right. We made the decision and I won't tell you more than I already have."

Let's look more closely at the long-term picture. What do you regard as the basic trends that will affect McCormick?

First, we don't think people will stop eating spices in the home. Spices have been an ingredient in the kitchen for a thousand years, and we think they're going to be there for another thousand.

We think foodservice is a real growth area. In restaurants, company cafeterias, and so on. Our research says that people are eating nearly one meal of every four away from home. That includes the fast-food outlets. We expect the figure to reach one meal in three by 1980.

Well, we looked at this trend for a long time, and we saw opportunities to meet a real need.

What was their need and your opportunity?

Restaurants waste a lot of products. They can't avoid it. It's costly. For example, you put the ketchup bottle on the table and it's used at a certain rate. When the bottle is half empty, there is a certain amount of loss. Salad dressing is an even better example. There's a lot left in the bowl after it's been served on the table. You can't serve the same container to another customer because of health regulations. So we put up ketchup and salad dressings in small individual portion packs. The packaging costs more, but the merchant saves money by eliminating wasted products.

Has your planning process detected other opportunities for growth? Or, to put it another way, have you spotted other needs?

Sure.

For instance?

Frozen foods. Packaged dinners. The way you flavor these things is entirely different and much more difficult than just putting on salt and pepper. We were sure we had the technology to help the food processors, the ones who supply frozen food dinners, the pot pies, that sort of thing. These foods are not cooked in the conventional way as you would cook at home. In the home kitchen, you put a flavoring into what you're cooking and this permeates the food gradually, while it's in the oven or cooking for an hour or two on the stove. But frozen dishes are prepared in an industrial fashion. They're cooked to whatever degree is necessary to make them a saleable product. Some of this is done, of course, for bacteriological reasons. But the conventional sprinkling-on of spices just isn't appropriate. So we get into the design of different kinds of flavorings. You don't have the time to cook slowly now; you're just going to heat the dish in your radar oven or a regular oven for thirty minutes. So you have to get the flavor out faster.

Therefore, instead of using natural spices, we take the oleoresins and the essential oils out of the spices. We put them on "carriers" of some sort, such as salt, and disperse them in other fashions.

Part of food's appeal is that it's visually attractive and has a pleasant aroma. That's why there's nothing more exciting than to walk past a bakery. If you do a frozen pie, pop it in the oven to warm it up, and it comes out smelling like a fresh bakery product, you've got a saleable product. We have the ability to encapsulate flavors and various "carriers" that won't release that flavor until it gets to a certain temperature. Then it's released quickly. There's a real market for our industrial flavor products here.

Do you foresee a trend toward natural foods—whatever that means? Will that affect your business?

I don't know how well I can respond to that, because I really don't understand the "natural food" business. I think a lot of people perceive it to be food that is grown without benefit of fertilizer or insecticide.

Isn't it broader than that? Many people talk about tomatoes, for example. They look beautiful, but they're tasteless. Hot-house grown.

Well, as far as I'm concerned, tomato ketchup tastes as good now to me as it did when I was a kid a long time ago. In the agricultural business, the onion and garlic business, we're breeding plants to accomplish certain ends. And although the character of some of the foods has changed over the years, I'm sure it's not been all for better nor all for worse. Selective breeding gets food to your home in useable condition at a lot lower cost than if we had merely just gone along as we had done at the turn of the century with the little truck farm located one day from the marketplace. We couldn't support our economy or our population today with that kind of farm supply. Today, you breed tomatoes to get tougher skins, because they must travel further. Lettuce is grown with different things in mind, again, to be able to get it to the marketplace in good condition.

We grow onions on the West Coast; we have some 10,000 acres planted. We have bred a variety of onion that is good for dehydrating, but it's not good if you want to slice it for your hamburger. It would take the top of your head off, it's so hot. But in the processing, we lose some of that. We're not able to hold all that flavor when we dehydrate. But when you use it at home as a dehydrated product, you're not very far from the natural onion in terms of the characteristics of an onion. It's been very well received.

Are public tastes changing in ways that will affect your market?
The changing tastes that we see largely revolve around "ethnic" foods. That's been very dramatic. Since the late 1930s and 1940s, there's been a tremendous increase in the use of herbs in cooking. We believe it's because since that period, a lot of people have traveled abroad and experienced foods in other locations. For example, American service personnel overseas, business people traveling, vacationers; they've been going to new areas. They try new kinds of foods and they like them.

This has created a new market for you.
Right. In the early 1940s, for example, the whole Italian cooking bit was relatively unknown in this country, except in small Italian-American neighborhoods. Today, I think there's hardly a US family that doesn't have something very Italian-oriented in its diet fairly frequently.

We see a similar trend coming on strong with Mexican foods, tacos, foods prepared with chili and chili powder.

You've been alert to find who needed your technology.
Not just technology. We were aware of another problem. In the food service and restaurant business, there is a tremendous tonnage of spice sold, pepper, chili powder, cinnamon, and so forth. You can't economically distribute these products alone. Freight costs are extremely high for small shipments. There are very few people who can buy packaged one-pound or five-pound spice containers by the truckload. And you go to LTL—less than truckload—and it gets very expensive. The smaller the quantity, the higher the rate. So we decided to look for products that would give us sufficient tonnage to take advantage of lower freight rates. We

looked in our sphere of things and asked ourselves what in the seasoning business could give us this kind of tonnage. And we made a major commitment, surely a strategy decision. We decided to go very heavily into supplying mayonnaise and salad dressing products to the foodservice trade. We've built a very substantial business as a result of that decision.

How long did it take before it started to pay off?
We've always been in the salad dressing business in a very minor way. We had the technology; we did a little retail business here in Baltimore for many years. But when we made this major commitment, it showed results within the first two years, and it's growing at a very rapid rate today.

Have you made other strategic decisions that have taken years to pay off?
Oh, yes. Our industrial flavor division has been doing research for years on flavorings other than the natural spices: oleoresins, encapsulation of flavors, spray drying.

And we do basic research in flavors and tastes. We spend a great deal of time taking natural flavors and breaking them down into their various chemical components.

Do you have a significant research budget?
A very large one. Large for us in terms of what we can support. Remember that in the food business, you are working with relatively low margins.

We don't expect quick payoffs. I would think—strictly a guess off the top of my head—that our payoff is really beyond five years, considering the total range of things we're involved in. I would say one thing about our research: it's not designed to develop an individual product. It's cumulative basic research. When we break down a natural flavor and learn how to use it to achieve certain results, we may not call on that for five years. But once we've learned something, we'll always have it in our bag of tricks.

So I guess you could say our research tends to be fairly basic, as opposed to finding specific formulas or products.

Looking beyond your own company, what are some of the broader issues you're concerned with? You've talked very forcefully in the past about the problem of government policies.

Yes, I believe that the achievements of both our country and McCormick are intrinsically tied to the free enterprise system, where profit—not governmental commands—is the motivation. The future depends on reducing the size of government and on successfully communicating the merits of our economic system. We're very committed to that goal.

But you're frustrated.

Yes. Business just isn't speaking out very effectively in its own defense. I think the reason is simply that you can't get the media attention you need in order to get the message across. You don't pick up the newspaper and read good news. You don't read about the good things business is doing. But have one product failure, one disenchanted person, and a reporter will pick it right up.

You have personal friends who are newspaper publishers, Harry. What do they say when you discuss your complaints about their news coverage?

I do tell them. You know what the answer is. "We don't really have control over what the writers put in the paper." I can't accept that, and I tell them that, too. It's as if I were to say I have no control over my employees, so if we were to send out shoddy merchandise, I'd be absolved of any responsibility. Ridiculous.

Newspapers and the other media are themselves big business, though. Certainly, papers like The Wall Street Journal *and magazines such as* Fortune *and* Forbes *are owned by people who are committed to the free enterprise system. They're not anti-business, yet they print articles critical of many aspects of business. What do you think can be done about it?*

I honestly don't know. I do think legitimate criticisms of business exist. So I guess what I'm saying is that a lot of the criticism seems to be reported out of proportion to its impact on the individual and the society.

Can you give me a case in point?

The automobile, which is definitely one of the most reliable machines that has ever been invented. You buy a new car and, 95 times out of 100, you can take it off the showroom floor and drive 55 miles per hour for the next 30,000 miles. But what do you read in the paper? All the problems. Not that they don't exist, but nobody points out that a lot of cars are running well; people are happy with them and they're highly reliable.

How much of this whole problem is just caused by inadequate or unfair news coverage? And how much results from the misbehavior of corporate management?

I really don't know. It's a very complex thing. I get as distressed as anyone when I hear that somebody has done something which reflects badly on all business. But not all business people are crooks, damn it. Ninety-nine percent of them are honest and hard-working. Yet there seems to be an attitude that business is doing everything wrong.

What is the toughest job you have as McCormick's chief executive officer?

Well, I don't think there are any easy ones. But in my opinion, the toughest single job is simply to keep people working together effectively. It sounds like motherhood, but that's the job: people. It's a people thing. You know, finance is tough, quality control is a big problem, government is a big problem. But the thing that impacts 100 percent on what you do is people. Keeping them working harmoniously and towards the same objectives is the greatest challenge.

Ellmore C. Patterson

Chairman and Chief Executive Officer
J. P. Morgan & Co. Incorporated

Ellmore C. Patterson occupies the same office, on the second floor of 23 Wall Street, New York, that once was the office of J. P. Morgan, Jr., who succeeded his father, J. Pierpont Morgan, as managing partner of the foremost banking firm of American industry.

At sixty-three, Mr. Patterson heads one of the largest banking enterprises in the world, respected for its skills in corporate and international banking, as well as for its integrity and leadership.

J. P. Morgan & Co. Incorporated, whose predecessor began business in 1862, is a holding company whose principal subsidiary, Morgan Guaranty Trust Company of New York, was formed in 1959 by merger of the Morgan bank with the Guaranty Trust Company of New York. That bank's origins date to 1839. For more than a century, Morgan Guaranty has operated in London and Paris, and its international experience and banking connections are unsurpassed. Today, the bank has assets exceeding $25 billion, and manages trust and advisory funds of more than $22 billion.

Mr. Patterson became president of the bank and the parent company in 1969, and was elected chairman of the board and chief executive officer of both in 1971. He originally joined J. P. Morgan & Co., then a private banking firm, in 1935, on graduation from the University of Chicago, where he was captain of the football team in his senior year. During World War II, he served in anti-submarine warfare aboard a destroyer escort in the Pacific.

Besides holding several corporate directorships, Mr. Patterson has been President of the Federal Advisory Council of the Federal Reserve System. He is a trustee of the University of Chicago, the Memorial Sloan-Kettering Cancer Center, and is a member of the Corporation of the Massachusetts Institute of Technology.

Mr. Patterson, you have a large number of officers in your middle management. I went through your annual report and counted something like 385 vice-presidents of the Morgan Guaranty Trust Company. And a large number of assistant vice-presidents, too.

You don't give out titles easily. These people get authority and responsibility to go with their officerships. They're the people from whom you'll draw your senior management in the future.

What do you look for when you size up these officers for growth potential in the bank?

First, I must see intellectual capacity. I don't say you have to be Phi Beta Kappa, but you do need a high order of intelligence. I also look for a kind of courage. Not arrogance, but the deeply-seated ability to stick by your convictions when they're being tested by your peers and your seniors. Integrity is also extremely important, of course.

How well can you size up a person in the early stages of his career with you?

Well, it's not easy. But if you're going to work with someone, you'd better be able to figure out pretty well ahead of time what he's like. Has he got tunnel vision? Will he take a broad or narrow view? Has he got the capacity to deal with clients—that sensitivity enabling him to detect different character, personality, and needs between people who may appear quite similar on the surface?

Would you explain that, Mr. Patterson?

He should be able to judge whether with one client he can put his cards on the table. Whether a client is coming square with him. Whether the client likes to trade. With one man, he can put his cards right on the table. With another man, it may take three or four meetings before you really get down to the facts. A banker should be able to judge those things.

Because he's there to make a deal. When you want to get something done, you have to be able to persuade him. This is the way you do things.

I don't know quite how to describe this. People are very different. We want to get people who have the ability to evaluate different people.

Those people aren't always easy to find.

There are some people whose performance records amount to straight A's all the way through, and they can tell you about all you want to know about anything. But they're not sensitive people and they don't understand priorities. Their abilities to handle personal relationships leave something to be desired.

Credentials aren't enough. The person has to make you believe in him?

Right. As I often say, you may think you're bright, but if you can't convince people of it, what good is it? Also, you may be an absolute genius, but if I don't sense that you've got an appetite for work, I'll have good reason to suspect that your talents may go down the drain. You have to be hungry for work not only from a monetary standpoint but from a simple desire to succeed.

Morgan has a reputation for having and developing men of independent judgment. How do you develop that talent, instead of bringing along "yes-men"?

Well, I strongly discourage "yessing" at any level, because I don't know all the answers and neither do other senior people. We don't want a situation where the juniors say, "I'll just collect information and let the senior make the decision." We don't want people to try something fancy to see how it flies with us. We want them to recommend decisions. We've tried to push this philosophy down through the organization. We want the juniors to speak up. We want them to be very well prepared. They know this is what we expect from them.

We make it clear to new employees from the start that there'll always be uncertain or unknowable factors in a situation. We want them to collect and consider all relevant information. But over-study can't substitute for decision-making.

You want decision-makers, or at least firm recommendations for a decision?

Right. And I don't want someone to simply give me a review of a situation he's studied for weeks and then expect me to render a decision in ten seconds flat. I've made it clear that anyone who comes to me on a business matter should first have tried mentally to wear my shoes. My final decision may not be in line with the recommendation but, as long as I see careful preparation and analysis, I won't react negatively to the individual.

In many cases, you delegate final decision-making to the junior level. What happens when they're wrong?

Well, in our business, we deal in percentages and predictions, so mistakes are inevitable. But we believe that we'll get good overall results if our decision-making is preceded by sound, conscientious study. So the means are as important to us as the ends. And our people know that if they make thoughtful, well-considered decisions, we'll accept the risks inherent in an uncertain world.

Still, it's quite a responsibility.

Yes, it is. A number of our fund managers oversee portfolios with total market values of around one billion dollars. That should give you some idea of the responsibility.

You've been doing an impressive job of bringing minorities and women into those sorts of positions.

Well, there's a lot more we've got to do, but I think we've made real strides. Our typical fund manager is still a white male, for instance, but we've now got several blacks and about nine women in those positions. We've also got four women vice-presidents. Overall, we have more than fifty women officers, including those who travel around the country and abroad representing the bank to corporations and so on. This was almost unheard of ten years ago.

How have the women and blacks worked out in these positions?

Oh, it's been an excellent experience. You know, we don't promote someone or give them a chance unless they're up to the standards of the bank; these people are capable. They've proven themselves. In terms of clients, Morgan's philosophy is that they hire the institution, Morgan Guaranty, rather than a particular loan officer or fund manager.

Are the minorities and women themselves getting used to it? Do you have any sense, for example, of how blacks feel about being in corporate banking?

I haven't had enough opportunity to really sit down with them, but when we do come in contact, they always seem to be enthusiastic, and proud of the fact that they're part of the bank. They're glad to belong to an organization that doesn't make distinctions on the basis of race or whatever. The only real problem we've had with minorities is that we've had trouble keeping some of the very best people. They're in such demand, and some of them even want to go out and start a bank of their own.

Why?

Because they feel that, for their group, it would be beneficial. They want to participate and contribute as much as possible.

You value ambition in your employees.

Yes, but as I tell everyone in this bank, "I won't promise you anything. Do your job well and your future will take care of itself. You've got nothing to worry about." You know, I think everyone looks around and wonders where they're going. But where you go depends on how good a job you do. I'm old-fashioned and I know it, but I think there's no substitute for the work ethic. That's what I value.

There are some geniuses who can get things done between 9 and 5. But I think the guy who spends more time at his work is going to be the best. He's the man I want.

I'm sure you practice what you preach. What time do you get to your office in the morning?

Oh, between 8:15 and 8:45. I never leave before 5:30 or 6:30. And of course, I do a lot of work in the evenings and so on.

Tell me what you do on a typical day.

There are no typical days, and there aren't many prearranged priorities. My daily calendar is probably the least routine part of my life. Of course, I always have clear priorities in terms of what I want to do first, but I don't plan it that way. I don't say that three-quarters of my time will be spent on the bank or whatever. I have to take it as it comes, because there are so many unexpected diversions.

Such as?

Well, my work with MAC (Municipal Assistance Corporation) during the New York City fiscal crisis. I cancelled trips to Europe, attendance at directors meetings, important meetings at the bank and so on, simply because the New York thing had a high priority as far as I was concerned.

How long did you spend on it?

It was never full-time. And I don't believe that I ever neglected the bank, because that was always my top priority and, if I couldn't be there, I made sure that someone I trusted was on hand. But there were pressure points. When MAC was created, for instance, we had three weeks of round-the-clock work. I wasn't there for all of it, but I did spend a good deal of time in meetings. And I spent a lot more just thinking about the situation and trying to come up with proposals.

It isn't only your physical presence at a meeting that counts. When you are playing golf, when you are doing anything, you're thinking about it all the time. I think that's just as important as the hours of the day that you sit in at a meeting.

I like to try to think ahead. I'ts terribly important to try to anticipate what may happen. I don't believe in worrying, but I do spend a lot of time trying to think ahead.

When you're in management, you are responsible for getting ahead of problems. You need to work out your options beforehand. So even when I wasn't at a particular meeting on the New York City problem, I was always thinking ahead as to what my committee might recommend.

The bank obviously has a large stake in the financial future of New York City. But when the relationship between Morgan and an activity is more tenuous, how do you decide where to spend your time? You must get a huge number of dinner invitations, for example.

During the banquet season, from October through March, I probably attend an average of two dinners a week, sometimes three. I try to identify the high priority occasions in terms of what is good for the bank. If it doesn't have to do with the bank but I personally like the people, I'll go anyway. It's that simple.

Two or three nights a week is a heavy schedule, Mr. Patterson.

Well, Mr. Burger, sometimes there's a week with none. I think that's good, because all of us like to spend time with our families. My first priority is my family. No question about that.

I think I've been able to carry out most of my objectives for my family without any major conflict. When I was made president of the bank, my youngest son, who was then eleven years old, said, "Good, Daddy, now you can come home once in a while." Well, Mrs. Patterson knows that something like the New York City crisis comes up once in a while, but I very rarely schedule any business meetings on weekends. And I don't like to go out three nights in a row.

You're very much concerned with how you use your time.

Surely. You can buy technology. You can attract capital. But we all have to operate within the confines of a 24-hour day. And development of people takes a lot of time.

That brings you to a paradox. The faster you expand, the more you need to develop new talent, and the less time you have to do it.

You must plan out your time to a large extent.

Yes, I've got a calendar listing major meetings and out-of-town affairs for the next year. And when I'm on trips, I have a little book that I live by. If I lost it, I don't know what I'd do. Looking through it, I can see at a glance what I've got scheduled in the coming weeks. And I know what I have to prepare for. I make sure I have gotten memos in advance to give me the background.

How far in advance is your time committed?

Well, right now I'm pretty well tied down next week. I have two days in Washington, then an all-day meeting here. After that, I've got a General Motors meeting in Detroit—I'm on their board—and an annual meeting in Chicago. After that, there's one day that I don't have a thing to do—so far.

Being out of town so much, how can you make sure that things continue to run smoothly here at the bank?

We have a corporate office which is made up of five of our top officers. Besides myself, it includes Mr. Page [the president], the executive committee chairman and two vice chairmen. And we're interchangeable in the sense that I'm comfortable with having any of them run the bank. If they're there, I know things will be okay. They're all very competent people. But, we don't leave only one man in charge for an extended period of time.

How often do you meet with them?

Twice a week. First, the five of us get together by ourselves. And then we meet with the division heads. We talk about the same things in both groups; the five of us meet alone simply because there may be things that we don't want to go out of our circle.

What do you discuss?

Well, it's loosely structured. Each of the five of us has his own areas of primary attention, and the meetings reflect that.

Then we have the division executive vice-presidents come in and meet with us. With them, basically we talk policy and major issues. We don't want to go into detail unless it's important. We touch on operations, personnel, the financial side, the legal side, the international side. But we consciously try to avoid setting rigid lines. And while the division heads each serve as chief executive officer of a particular function, they're being trained to think in a broader frame all the time. They participate in bank-wide decision-making.

Do you have a policy of deliberately shifting executives from one area to another to broaden their experience?

Yes. You might call it musical chairs. We'll bring a man back from Europe and put him in a responsible position over here. And vice versa. The principal shifting has been between the national and international banking operations, but it's not restricted to that. We shift people in and out of operations.

Incidentally, we have practically no interchange with the Trust Investment department. There's generally a brick wall there.

But if there's a young man in general banking who doesn't seem to cotton to that, for example, we might tell the trust investment division that he's ripe for a change. If we think he's good, they'll take it from there.

Okay. Getting back to these meetings with your division heads, do you have an agenda worked out in advance?

No, but I generally have things that I want to talk about, and so do the others. We all have things we want to point out, policy considerations we want to bring up. Or sometimes, we may talk over just a small matter or a funny incident. We get along very well together.

Do you vote?

No, never. But when we finish talking about something, we'll know the consensus. We can't fully operate on a partnership basis because of the size and variety of the decisions, but we retain that informal feeling. When it comes to major policy questions and things like that, we may talk, go away and think about it, come back and talk again.

And you come to an agreement?

Right. It may not be unanimous but, after all the talk, we often get pretty close to that.

As chief executive officer, though, you make the final decisions?

Ellmore C. Patterson

Yes, but we try to operate on a basis where I tell them exactly what I feel and they do the same with me. I level with them, and I expect them to tell me exactly what they feel. In other words, my corporate officers and division heads aren't going to automatically agree with me or say something just to make me happy.

Sometimes, I go into a meeting with a position. I'll try it out on them. This is hardly an inside "family secret;" I don't usually have to ask them what they think. But sometimes, I'll propose something, and if there's silence, I'll say, "Wait a minute. I want to talk about this. I don't want you just to accept it." Sometimes, I like to drag in far-out ideas which they haven't thought about. I want them to think about them.

I try to look at the whole society. Not only the competition, but business generally, politics, legislation. I try to keep tuned in. Of course, I'm not the only one who does. All of the senior fellows are thinking in a broad way, too. But I consider my distinct responsibility to equate this bank with what's going on outside. We discuss these things. Sometimes, when we have big issues, we'll just take the day off to talk about them.

It's unstructured. But it's a style we feel comfortable with, and a style we have lived with. And I try to keep it as unstructured as possible.

Let's shift gears here, because I want to talk about your work as a director. You're a Director of General Motors, Standard Brands and two other companies. I wonder how much time you spend on this work.

It depends on the complexity and program of the corporation. But generally, it's about half a day per month plus preparation, which can mean another two to six hours of solid reading and maybe telephoning. You always have papers to study before a meeting and so on. I would say that 100 percent of the preparation isn't done on office time, though. I do it when I'm traveling or commuting, mostly.

But it's a lot of work.

Yes, and the meetings are getting longer. There's more time spent on the various subcommittee reports, for one thing. And there's been all this

licity about business, its products, its contributions and all that.
natural, in that environment, for directors to want to closely
these publicized areas.

What do you learn from your experience on these boards?

Well, I think anyone who's in a policy-making position will have an extremely limited view if he just sits in his office, looks at his own figures and reads the newspaper. It's terribly important to have varied experience in major management. You know, in the broad sense, the problems of corporations are pretty much the same. But everyone approaches them differently.

And you think it's important to know how the other guy does it?

Right. How are the decisions made? What's the organizational set-up? How does strategic planning work? I don't say it's impossible to get this information if you're not a director. But as a director, you live with it and you sit in on conversations. And it's very helpful.

How do you feel about your younger officers accepting corporate directorships?

I think it has to be clearly understood by everyone in this bank that if they accept a directorship, they are on their own. They are not representing the bank. They must make sure that no information in relation to the corporation passes from them to this bank, even though we do business with the company involved. If they accept the directorship, they keep their own fees. They serve on their own time.

But we encourage them. We think it's definitely broadening for them to get out and learn the problems of another industry. And from their experience at the bank, they should be able to bring to that board the ability to be a watchdog or an idea man, or whatever, whether in the field of economics or finance.

Mr. Patterson, you try to give your officers and staff a sense of belonging, a sense of proprietorship. Have you been successful?

Well, I am modest by nature. But excuse me for saying I think we have done a very good job. I hear this from clients, from competitors, from our own people that we have created an intimate family. The employees of this bank have loyalty and pride.

We have high standards in this bank. We have quality we can be terribly proud of. Fortunately, we inherited this, and I don't think we have tarnished it. I think we have improved it.

This is what I tell our people: "People are what makes the show run. Keep plugging."

Ellmore C. Patterson

45

Robert W. Galvin

*Chairman of the Board
and Chief Executive Officer*
Motorola, Inc.

When Paul V. Galvin founded Motorola in 1928, its assets consisted of just $565 and a tiny Chicago workshop. Less than fifty years later, the company records $1.5 billion in annual sales and employs 50,000 people in plants and offices around the globe.

The firm, which introduced the first commercial car radio in 1929, used that innovation as a springboard for launching numerous other enterprises. As a result, Motorola is today a recognized leader in semiconductor and automotive products; communications, defense and space electronics equipment.

In addition, the company has recently made auspicious entries into such fields as components for timepiece electronics and display products for data systems.

Robert W. Galvin, who joined his father's firm in 1944, has headed Motorola since 1956. A strong advocate of education, he attended the University of Notre Dame and the University of Chicago. He is a trustee of the Illinois Institute of Technology, a director of Junior Achievement of Chicago, and one of twelve Fellows of the University of Notre Dame. The impetus he provided led to the creation of Motorola's Executive Institute, which gives the firm's managers an opportunity to renew their intellectual pursuits.

How does your management really get beneath the figures to learn what's really happening in your various divisions?

Good figures do tell us a great deal of what's going on. By "good figures," I mean not just the bottom line, the summaries, but enough detailed data for us really to understand the substance. Of course, if they're to be useful, we need a good base to compare them with. For instance, comparable figures for recent periods. From this, we can see the trends. We can see in what directions the division is going. And, if we're still not satisfied, we can ask intelligent questions.

But figures aren't always enough, Bob.

No, that's true. You need an objective environment. You need an environment that's open, where you have good and honest communications with your managers. You need an atmosphere where they share information with top management regularly, the good and the bad.

Plus detailed and regular reports?

Of course. We expect qualitative reports from our managers. We get them regularly. We don't like surprises. It's part of our philosophy here that middle management and division management must share with us information early. They've got to anticipate what ultimately might happen. We expect them to alert us even before anything shows up in the quantitative reports.

How do you arrange the right setting to get this kind of informal information—advisory warnings, if you will?

I believe we in top management must circulate. We try to attend regular formal meetings. But that isn't enough. We circulate informally. We observe closely. Once in a while, we pick up a coincidental piece of information that stimulates us to dig a bit deeper.

I emphasize listening. All of us in top management learn to do a lot of that. We have, I suppose, a very low level of toleration for rationalization. We strive to hear what other people want us to hear, even though they don't always come out and say it directly. It's our job to appraise it objectively.

When you do find a problem, how do you go about correcting it? How do you cut through the layers and do something about it?

Well, when we discover a problem, or think we may have discovered a problem, the first thing we do is to work with the incumbent management to acknowledge that there is indeed a problem. Only then can we try to define it precisely.

Of course, if we identify the true problem, and the divisional management won't acknowledge it, we've got another problem on our hands. Then we may need a radical organization change. But if the incumbent management demonstrates its objectivity, and shows us they're fully conscious of the problem, then we cut through the layers by working directly with them to solve it.

Sometimes, I like to mix levels of management. In that way, we make sure that all levels are being heard, and nobody is with-holding information. Even when there's full trust between levels of management, sometimes we find it desirable to go directly to the customers or employees where the problem is most evident. In that way, we can directly feel, sense, and understand the problem the way they do. And they're most directly involved, so they see it most clearly.

If we've got a really serious problem, sometimes we must order concrete action from the top. But we'd much prefer to have the directions emanate from a lower level, and that's the way it happens most often.

You want to cut down on executive politics?

Exactly. Because when we're comparatively free of politics, we start to see a spirit of disciplined candor. We're honest with each other. And each individual is honest with himself. We're objective, and we can direct our energies toward getting the job done.

In the larger sense, I believe that if we can create an environment where everyone can be reasonably objective, we're going to get the most and best from them. They'll be trying to solve problems, not defend themselves.

My experience, Bob, is that people tend to cover up failures for two reasons. One, they're afraid of losing their jobs if they admit there's a problem. Even more important, people just don't like to admit that they've been wrong. As chairman, you can afford to face mistakes without these worries. But what about the people down the line? How do you get real honesty from them?

The way we treat people encourages them to be candid. If a man or woman attempts to shield us from a problem or mistake, for instance, we will ultimately find out, and he or she will get a most significant reprimand. If it happens again, they might also be dismissed.

If someone continually makes mistakes, of course, there's no place for him here. But we're talking about the top 300 or 400 people, and they're smart enough to do most things well.

My father, who founded our company, probably summed it up. "I don't mind a man who is occasionally dumb," he used to say, "but I can't stand a man who is numb."

What exactly did he mean?

He didn't mind a person who made a mistake, who just plain forgot to think something through or who made an error in judgment of some kind. But if the fellow was so numb as to be unwilling to either recognize or correct a problem, he didn't stay here very long. I probably make this point three or four times a year, because I think it's a significant principle in establishing a management environment where people can contribute all they've got to give.

We've been talking about candor within the corporation. I'm curious about your feelings on disclosure to stockholders and the business community in general. Before the Securities and Exchange Commission required you to break a percentage of the business into separate divisions, it was possible for a corporation to bury its shortcomings, right? I'm not saying that Motorola did this, but it would be much harder now, wouldn't it?

Yes, if you wanted to bury your shortcomings, it was a lot easier in those days.

I might add that we here consider it desirable even now to keep much of that discreet information reasonably private—for competitive reasons, not because we're trying to shield ourselves from the analysts or our other publics. I certainly agree that there has to be adequate disclosure, but that doesn't necessarily mean that the bureaucrat's judgment as to what constitutes adequate disclosure is always correct.

Let me move on to a very sensitive area. You have a plant in South Korea, a country whose government doesn't seem to put much value on freedom. Are there any political, social or ethical problems in an area that's devoid of freedom?

It's a complex issue. You have to balance the good and bad and then decide what, in your judgment, is right. In regard to Korea, I made that analysis over a decade ago and I'm still comfortable with it today. I think South Korea's strength is very important to preservation of the free world, though I recognize that the present government there is far less free in civil and political rights than we'd like.

The prospect of leaving the unbalancing of power in that region to others' devices, in other words, is a much larger risk to world freedom than is Korea's internal situation. So, in my judgment, it's a proper foreign policy for the United States to aid South Korea; and it's proper to support that policy and for companies like Motorola to help preserve the balance of power between South and North Korea.

And you feel that Motorola's presence is similarly productive?

We're not there overtly to support the Park regime. Everybody in the US would like to see Mr. Park head a different government situation. But he's there. He exists. And, as a matter of fact, the South Korean people have far superior civil rights compared to North Korea. In our opinion, the 4,000 people who work for us there are far better off than if Motorola wasn't in Korea.

In what ways?

They're better off economically. They're eating better. Their health is better. Their schooling is better. I might add that healthy, intelligent people will find ways to work out their problems for themselves; whereas unhealthy, ignorant people will always be subjugated. And I think it's reasonable to postulate that, a generation or two from now, things will be a whale of a lot better in South Korea. At least this way, they have the potential.

Speaking of your worldwide operations, you've really made impressive strides with Motorola. When you took over from your father, sales were just a fraction of what they are now.

Well, my father allowed me to share in the leadership of the corporation starting about 1950, at which time we were doing about $100 million in sales. By 1958, when my father became inactive, I think we were up around $200 million. Today, we're approaching $1.5 billion.

So you've pushed it to between five and ten times what it was when you began to take over?

I've assisted in the creation of, and supported an environment where a group of people could accomplish that. I presume there have been a few corporations where a couple of people could say, "This is what I did." In this case, there were very few things that I alone caused to happen. What I did do, I think, was to cause a lot of people within the institution to perceive opportunities and discover that they were supported.

You know, I've always felt that a very significant responsibility of a chief executive of a corporation is simply to spread hope.

General Doriot, of American Research and Development Corporation in Boston, told me that was one of his major tasks.

It sounds vague and general, but it isn't. When things aren't going so well, a chief executive has to seek opportunities to provide support and courage. That has been very useful for me to remember. It's substantive. Institutions have to believe in the future. And they have to be substantive, not rhetorical.

That reminds me of something that AT&T's Director of Corporate Planning Research, Hank Boettinger, once wrote. He said that if you told the inventors of the transistor in 1948 that they'd be responsible for the end of African colonialism, they'd say, "You're crazy. What are you talking about? We've invented a device to switch phone calls more efficiently." But as Boettinger pointed out, transistors led to transistor radios, which brought the outside world to remote African villages where there was no electricity. For the first time, through their radios, the people were exposed to nationalism, which eventually awakened Africa and put an end to the colonial empires.

In other words, the scientists were developing a new technical device to improve the switching of telephone calls. But they ended up changing the world. You've talked about looking at the future, at the broad picture. Are your people doing that?

Well, I think 99 percent of our time is devoted to pragmatic applications, to engineering questions, getting better yields, and so on. And I think, frankly, that the only way the world is going to solve its problems is if everyone carries his grain of sand, so to speak. If we're all dealing in grand concepts all the time, we won't have the resources to get anywhere.

As managers, we consciously spend perhaps one percent of our time being concerned with the grand event, to the limited degree that we're able to perceive it. But if we were to sit up here and try to be great philosophers, then we wouldn't be doing our job.

Although much of our work is fairly mundane, we certainly see the relevance of it to our society. Suppose we had an unusual new antenna system. We would recognize its tremendous impact on the defense of freedom. We would recognize that if we have this and the Soviets don't have it, it may be a significant advantage for us. Who knows, we may be able to help preserve freedom. In my estimation, freedom is our highest priority.

If we make a product, a tool, that provides answers to some of the problems of our society, I think that's very significant. That's the broad view we take.

And, in an atmosphere like that, if I can help to create a climate where people will perform above average, our future will take care of itself.

How do you create such a climate?

By starting with a respect for everyone's dignity and by accenting the positives. In other words, we really try to emphasize the building of a man's or woman's strengths. We don't put too much emphasis on weaknesses, except to try to cause a person to strive for improvement.

When you hire somebody, what "strong points" do you particularly look for?

Integrity. Intelligence. Heart or empathy. Does the person have the courage to express his intelligence, and the courage to admit mistakes? I also look for vision, which to me means the ability to see the whole picture. You know, it's entirely possible to add up a lot of facts in a very intelligent way and still not see their relationship to each other. It's important, because facts are often brought together for the purpose of making a decision. The hard part is to be able to recognize which ones are significant.

Anything else?

I wonder if the man or woman has a spirit for leadership.

What does that mean?

Drive, desire, motivation. Somebody who really wants to be a leader. There are people entrusted with leadership positions who don't really want those positions. And there are many people who don't want to be leaders, so they never even try. The spirit of leadership is the desire to achieve power.

Suppose you were screening candidates for a senior executive position. How would you determine whether that person had the abilities and characteristics you've mentioned?

I'd look for signs in many ways. For example, I'd start by going back to the person's schooling. Did he run for office in school? Edit the newspaper? Or did he finish class at three o'clock every day, get a "B" on everything, and spend his time around the Coke machines? In other words, did the person reach out to try to influence his destiny or did he just settle for what was imposed on him?

A number of years ago, a Bell System study showed no significant correlation between a college man's extracurricular activities and his later success. The only correlation involved his grades, and the Bell theory was that, if you don't work hard in college, there's no reason to assume you'll suddenly start working on the job. How do you feel about that?

It makes some sense to me, but I would respectfully suggest that there is some insight to be gained by asking, "Have you ever aspired to any other leadership position before?" We don't want the man or woman who, at age forty, says, "No, I've never led anything in my life, but I sure would like to."

If he's really interested in leadership, he should have already had a lot of experience with it?

Yes, which is why I'm a supporter of such activities as Junior Achievement. It allows youngsters to discover that there *is* a thing called "leadership." You know, maybe nobody ever told them about it. Maybe they didn't have a father like mine who could show them by example that it's fun to be a leader. They get into Junior Achievement and suddenly, "Hey, I can be a secretary of this company. I can have some influence, and that's fun." If a kid has a spark for leadership, Junior Achievement or early job experiences can put him on a good track.

Let's get back to your whole emphasis on getting the most from people. I'd like to talk about your deferred profit-sharing plan, which seems to have been designed with that philosophy in mind.

It goes back to recognizing the dignity of the individual. The theory is that we can motivate people to be more loyal, hard-working, thoughtful and all the other characteristics that one has to have in a company. We'd like our people to have the prospect of taking home not only a salary, but also something extra at the end of the line.

The deferred part is what interests me most.

Well, there are a variety of benefits to doing it that way. For one thing, people earn more, because there's interest on the capital. Also, they're really investing in society, because profit-sharing money is turned around to provide investment funds. So we're providing a security for our employees, demonstrating our responsibility to them, and doing something good for society in general at the same time.

Bob, let's assume I were an hourly worker who'd been with Motorola for twenty-five years. What would my share of the deferred profit-sharing plan be worth?

The benchworker who started about twenty-five years ago would have an account book value of about fifty thousand dollars.

Really? That's extraordinary.

Well, it is. I have to say, there are a couple of companies that outrank us in this regard. But we're certainly in the ball park in terms of progress for people in this area. Our plan, you know, is biased in favor of the lower-paying jobs.

Why?

It stems from the philosophy of trying to make sure that everybody has a chance to earn a good deal.

Just to digress a minute. One time I was talking to General Wood at Sears Roebuck and somehow we got to talking about profit-sharing.

I asked him how he happened to start it at Sears Roebuck, and he said, "Well, I looked around and saw some of the older companies where one or two guys had decided they were going to get very rich. I didn't like that. To me, profit-sharing presented an opportunity for a lot of people to become sort of well-off.

"The consequence of that philosophy," General Wood told me, "was t I became very rich." Bread cast on the waters.

In a speech a few years ago, you said that people ought to work perhaps ten months of the year, have a month's vacation and go to school for a month. As with your profit-sharing plan, this seems to be inspired by the desire to get people to work up to their full capacity.

That's true. What I had in mind was a renewal process: a month for rest and a month for recharging. I think people clearly need some recreational time. And I'd like to see everyone have four weeks, which is what we give our longer-service employees. I also think it would be very desirable if most senior people had a couple of weeks here and there where they really went off and formally recharged themselves intellectually in a fashion that would relate to the business.

Assuming that most of your executives already hold undergraduate or grad school degrees, why do you consider the continuing annual education to be so important?

I think college is great. Students are exposed to the widest reaches of human vision. But what happens when they get out of school? The conventional business world treats them as if their entire mental interests and needs were bounded by the dimensions of their current job assignments. Then, as they enter positions of larger responsibility, they are supposed to suddenly expand their vistas. Well, by then it may be impossible. There is the danger of becoming intellectually dormant or narrow, just as a person is about to enter the major take-off phase of his career. This is why we established the Motorola Executive Institute.

Tell me a little about it.

Well, it's located on a large site outside of Tucson, Arizona. It's a specially built school which includes dorms and recreational facilities. We send each middle and upper management person there at least once, for four weeks. And I think there ought to be more of it. They study very sophisticated subjects.

Management? Technology?

Everything from anthropology to a day and a half on monetary exchange rates. Quite a bit on human relations subjects: philosophy, sociology. There's a unit on executive health, both mental and physical. Purely factual material is de-emphasized in favor of courses that address attitudes, values and motivations.

So you're really practicing what you preach in terms of educating employees.

Yes, we're practicing it here. You know, I think it will get to the point where companies will just tell managers or key contributors to figure out what they want to do for one month. It's got to be useful and substantive but not to be directly related to making a profit. Rather, to make the employee a better thinker or leader or person.

What about you? What if you could take more time off for study?

Oh, I think I'd emphasize areas like biology, electronics, physics and chemistry. I'vc got a lot to learn on those subjects. History, too. I'll never be satisfied that I know enough.

Peter G. Scotese

*President and Vice Chairman and
Chief Executive Officer*
Springs Mills, Inc.

Springs Mills, which has been headquartered in the little town of Fort Mill, South Carolina since its 1888 founding, ranks among the nation's largest textile manufacturers. Through acquisition of Seabrook Foods, the firm also is a significant producer of frozen foods under the Seabrook Farms and other labels. Annual sales by Springs Mills, which employs 20,000 people in twenty-nine textile and frozen food plants, exceed $500 million.

A former chairman of the board of the Milwaukee Boston Stores Division of Federated Department Stores, Inc., Peter G. Scotese was elected as Springs Mills' first non-family president in 1969. Named later as the firm's vice-chairman, he has since also become Springs Mills' chief executive officer.

In collaboration with Chairman of the Board H. William Close, he has installed a formal program of long-range planning that emphasizes profit orientation and management by objectives. Among this program's most important results have been the acquisition of Seabrook and the establishment of a $3 million research and development center.

Mr. Scotese has played a leading role in American industry. He is a member of the Board of Trustees and the Executive Committee of the American Management Association, and is vice-president-at-large of the AMA. He is a director of Bell & Howell, Gardner-Denver and Armstrong Rubber.

Scotese, who believes that a chief executive must keep abreast of social and cultural trends, maintains particularly strong alliances with the art world. An avid collector of original art, he is a trustee of the Fashion Institute of Technology (New York) and a contributing member of both the American Federation of Art (Chicago) and the Museum of Modern Art (New York).

You've often stressed the need for chief executives to be sensitive to cultural, social and technological changes in the world at large. Why do you consider this to be so important?

Because the contemporary chief executive has two options. Depending on how sensitive he is to what's happening in the world around him, he can make change his partner—or his executioner.

If I'm aware of cultural trends, changing consumer needs and so on, I'll be rewarded in terms of increased profits, a better competitive stature and a better ability to attract capital and human resources. If I fail to recognize and deal with change, on the other hand, I stand to lose more than a few dollars or a notch in the competitive rankings. I could lose a product, an entire market or even the company itself.

What sorts of societal changes have been important to your company, Pete?

Well, for one thing, the trend toward more leisure time, which has led to a more casual look in fashion.

I'll give you another example. Until about five years ago, the whole retail store focus was on "trading up." Raising the consumer's tastes in fashion. Moving him from the basement fashion lines to higher quality, higher-priced items to sell more goods at much greater profit.

I think that trend has run its course. You know, I used to be with Federated Department Stores in Milwaukee. And I remember walking through one of our leased departments there. We had a pet shop where we were selling an imitation diamond-studded collar for dogs. And I said to myself, "Next year, how do we trade up from that?" I think the world has been telling us lately that you go down or sideways, not up, from there; that conspicuous consumption is unnecessary, frivolous, almost immoral.

By today's standards?

Yes. And more particularly, by future standards. A third of the world is starving to death. And this country is utilizing the world's resources at a hell of a rate to support its standards of living. And its tastes.

Conspicuous consumption?

Partly conspicuous and partly just thoughtless. And it's damaging not just because it depletes the world's supplies, but because it's unhealthy for the individual. We need a good dose of moral restraint. The willingness to do without some things. The trend away from it, I might add, is very significant in that it will affect everyone in business, in the home, government, in the church. Everyone.

How will corporate profits be affected?
I think they'll be reinvested more judiciously. There will still be an emphasis on getting an adequate return on invested capital. But an adequate return may not mean an excessive one.

When you suggest that capital will be reinvested more judiciously, you're apparently talking about getting a better return on investment. But if you're going to be downgrading rather than upgrading frivolous items like the dog collar you mentioned, where is the better return going to come from?
I don't think the two are associated. You can cut out diamond-studded dog collars without cutting your return.

Let me put it another way. By our living standards, food, clothing, shelter and even transportation are considered basic necessities. But you'll find some frivolous items within those categories.

Compare today's automobile with the ones of twenty years ago, for example. Both of them will get you where you want to go, but today's is much more luxurious. My point is that, within the universe of transportation possibilities, you can identify both realistic and created needs. And I think the concentrated effort—in that and other industries—may shift more toward the real ones.

What effect has this perception had on your own company?
Let's look at one of our basic commodities. Every year, in one of our divisions, we make 350 million linear yards of fabric. And we sell it to home fashions and apparel fashions manufacturers for an average price of under $1 per yard. More expensive fabrics are available, of course, and they do sell in significant quantities. But we've found that, in most cases, the consumer will be satisfied with the product that's made with dollar-a-yard fabric. She may not get the same amount of psychic pleasure, but she can satisfy a real need at a relatively moderate price. And if we satisfy those real, fundamental needs in volume, our return will be better.

In general, is she getting a lower quality item in exchange for the lower price?
No. Take a look at the common bed sheet. Ten years ago, you could

buy it in white only, in cotton only, and you had to iron it. Today, for almost the same price, you get a polyester/cotton blend. It's printed; it lasts three times as long; and it never has to be ironed because we've added permanent press. A far better value.

I think that that kind of improved product is highly desirable in today's environment, and I think we'll see more of it. There will be less emphasis on gimmickry and on keeping up with Joneses. There'll be more concern with quality at a price.

Nobody would object to better bed sheets, but what happens when world needs mandate a change that the consumer isn't ready for? For example, Peter, we need shorter cars to conserve energy supplies, but there are signs that the public may still be demanding the bigger models.

This may sound pretty far out, but I wouldn't be upset if the length of cars were legislated. In other words, don't always give the people what they want. Give them what's right for most of the people most of the time. We do that already with other kinds of legislation.

What do you have in mind?

Well, for example, we've got OSHA (Occupational Safety and Health Act) and ERISA (Employees Retirement Income Security Act). The thrust of those laws is that the public interest requires restrictions on the employer. He has to meet certain minimum standards to assure that workers are protected against occupational hazards and in terms of pension rights. We've also got an endless array of consumer legislation.

So why not laws to protect the environment? If small cars are needed to assure an energy supply for the US as a whole, why not legislate it so that people can only buy cars within certain size limitations?

Well, let me play devil's advocate, Pete. If I want a diamond-studded collar or an overly long, gas-guzzling car, why not let me be a fool and engage in conspicuous consumption? Wouldn't it be better to regulate through economics rather than through legislation? In other words, for example, why not just discourage people from buying the frivolous items by making them more and more expensive?

I have two responses to that, because diamond-studded dog collars don't really affect society, but big gas-guzzling cars do.

If people want diamond-studded dog collars, therefore, maybe we should make them available. And we should charge a hell of a price, tax the hell out of them, and try to get some benefit for society from that kind of frivolous purchase.

I'm more reluctant to say that we should give people the freedom to buy that big car, but if we could tax it so that the community really benefited from the purchase, maybe I'd go along. I think I'd prefer that direction instead of legislation.

On the whole, though, you differ from many chief executives in your willingness to accept social legislation. A common conception is that it's all a great plot to disrupt the free enterprise economy.

I may be different because I don't see the alternative as being better. I don't think that, if we let the free marketplace prevail completely, it will necessarily cause the consumer to accept what's best for everybody. You know, human nature will always have its selfish side. And in many cases, legislation is the best, most expedient means of reaching the goal.

Let's look for a minute at OSHA. Critics have said that it focuses wholly on physical safety standards as opposed to safety education. One executive reports, therefore, that, while OSHA now has thousands of inspectors, the accident rate hasn't decreased even one-tenth of one percent. But you're expressing a good deal of confidence in the power of legislation and regulation.

My confidence is in enlightened legislation, and I don't think OSHA falls into that category. I agree that OSHA deemphasizes safety education, and that's unfortunate.

In a lot of cases, incidentally, I think accident prevention is the cheapest, most effective course. The entire population, for example, pays an incredible premium for fabrics which, as a result of legislation, are required to be flame-proof. They're paying to protect the very small number of people who, largely through carelessness, are burned. I think the money, in that case, would be infinitely better spent on prevention.

Okay. Let's turn to ERISA. That legislation certainly filled an important need to curb abuses in employee pension plans. But I've now seen many organizations, small ones particularly, trying to discontinue their pension plans entirely rather than cope with the perils of conforming to ERISA. Has the cure been worse than the problems? Or do you feel, Pete, that the legislation inspires your confidence more than the freedom and evils of a free market?

Well, my experience tells me that there have been some very fundamental abuses in the pension system. We've seen examples of it in the
Teamsters Union fund. So I think there's a crying need for more legislation, but I believe that ERISA went too far.

*Okay. You're not fully satisfied with either OSHA or ERISA. In light
of those acts, do you really feel confident that Congress or administrative
agencies can develop legislation to effectively limit wasteful energy consumption?*

I'm not sure. But if it can't be done expeditiously in the free marketplace, which so far seems to be the case, then it's going to have to be
legislated. I don't think we have a choice. It won't be a question of whether
or not I like it. What matters is that the free marketplace hasn't produced
significant results.

*When that legislation comes, what can be done to assure that it will
be more enlightened than, say, ERISA?*

Well, I think the problem with ERISA resulted largely from the fact
that business wasn't heard adequately in advance of the legislation's
enactment. Its message wasn't presented forcefully enough or wasn't
picked up enough by Congress.

*In general, how important do you think it is for business to maintain
a dialogue with the politicians who make state and national policy?*

Well, I think that that sort of communication can produce solutions
to the problems we've been discussing. With regard to preserving and
improving the quality of life, dialogue between business and the political
sector can help to determine when legislation is needed and what forms it
should take. Government has become such a big part of our lives that it's
vitally important to talk with legislators and government agencies.

Do you talk often to political figures?

Absolutely. Also, incidentally, we've added a new public affairs committee within our board of directors to help us manage our relationships
with government and to demonstrate a positive approach toward our responsibilities in areas involving government. And we've recently established a corporate public affairs committee for the same reasons.

*I've found that many chief executives don't take the time to talk to
politicians.*

Well, in many parts of the country, particularly urban ones, the obstacles to having a dialogue with a national or even state representative are awesome. But we're headquartered in the South, and I think the dialogue is more open there. The politicians make themselves more accessible to employers in this region, partly because they realize the significance of the payrolls we produce and so on. In fact, politicians listen well to all their constituencies in the South.

Throughout your career, Pete, you've maintained close ties not only with the political sphere, but with the cultural world as well. And you've said that the art world, in particular, is an excellent place to spot new trends. Why do you feel that way?

Because the contemporary artist is a terrific observer of what's going on in the world. The artist hits you with trial balloons of trends in the making. He's a window to the future, a barometer of changing attitudes. When artists began to express outrage at the Vietnam war, for example, that told me that there was a greater feeling of rage in the country than was then being communicated in the print and broadcast media. And when people like Andy Warhol made their statements about neon and plastic, they were saying, "Hey, it's a plastic world. It's become a very commercial world."

What conclusions do you derive from such statements?

Artists usually leave me with questions rather than conclusions. You know, if there's this much feeling in the art, is the world in fact becoming too commercial? Was the Vietnamese thing an outrage? Should we stop and reassess?

Then, through something personal, you do reassess. I remember driving through Phoenix, recalling how it once looked and how it looked now, with all the fast-food stands and gas stations. If I hadn't seen this so much in paintings by our contemporary artists, I might not have been observant of this. And so I had to wonder whether this is the kind of thing that the government and individual should support. And I thought, "Hey, let's slow down some of this."

Could that feeling influence your thoughts about plant design, signage or whatever?

It already has, as a matter of fact. We've gone to an all new, more uniform look in Springs Mills, including signage. Very low-key, less blatant and commercial. We've made an effort to properly landscape around our plants. We've put art on our plant and office walls and sculpture in the lobby to develop a more aesthetic appeal. And look at our new annual report, which includes a very tasteful series of photographs of South Carolina. That report isn't just numbers. It's a work of art, something that people will go through and appreciate.

Besides looking at paintings, how do you keep up with cultural and intellectual trends?

I watch what they're saying on TV, on Broadway and in Hollywood, in the music world and so on. There are environmental signals in all those places. I also go through about forty publications regularly. Some straightforward business material, some from the arts, and some more esoteric stuff from both fields.

What do you look for when you read?

Nothing specific, but I may pick up some small detail that keeps popping up in different places. When that happens, I'll get curious and wonder whether a trend isn't developing. In the art world, for instance, there's an upcoming interest in photography as an art form. You don't see significant evidence of it in any one place. But if you sift through a lot of material, you see little indications here and there. So you've got to believe there's a momentum gathering.

Do you think that trend might have some direct impact on your business?

Well, I see a trend that extends beyond something as elementary as photography as an art form. In fashion, for example, it involves a change from the completely-leisure look to a bit more formalism in dress. Already, the leisure suit is dead and the vested three-piece suit is in, for example.

Where do you detect this change?

In advertisements, in magazines, in the broadcast media. And in what I personally observe on the street. I sense just a bit more formality in hair style, in dress and so on. And look at what's happening to restaurants. Somebody spent four million dollars turning Tavern On the Green in New York City into a highly formalized place. It's happening elsewhere, too.

So I think there's definitely a renewed interest in formality. I'm not saying that it's going to overwhelm the world, just that people may have had too much of the dirty patch denim look. A backlash might be developing.

Could this affect your company's products somewhere down the line?

Yes, but we're talking about something that might take years to develop. With rare exception, I don't think any of these trends happen overnight or quickly enough so we'd be caught short. But a change like this might affect a point of view we have about making capital expenditures in certain areas, for example. We might think about going into denim or investing in coarse yarn goods and wind up saying, "No, I don't think so. It's running its course. Let's be cautious." It would be a subjective judgment, a gut-level decision.

Do you detect cultural trends that might affect industries other than your own?

Sure. For instance, everyone talks about recycling bottles and automobiles. Well, I see a lot of evidence toward recycling of household items like furniture and appliances. Flea markets are coming back in a big way, and they sell used household objects of every size, shape and description.

In some cases, people are even recreating turn-of-the-century household objects because demand has chewed up the available supply. And they feel it's cheaper and better to remodel and reuse something old than to go out and buy something new.

Ceiling fans are coming back, for instance, not because they're decorative, but because they're practical. They use a lot less energy, and they're efficient and cheap. That's just a small example, but I think there's a significant trend toward recycling more than bottles and cans.

How will it affect business?

It will cut into sales of new products in some fields, but not significantly. It will also create new business. Now that people are rediscovering the practicality of the ceiling fan, for example, they may go back and recreate a whole industry.

I'd like to ask you about a trend I've noticed. When you built your Elliott plant, only about eight percent of the machinery was purchased abroad. Whereas, more recently, you've been buying about 70 percent of your equipment from foreign sources. Why do you think you're not getting what you want from American industry?

That's an important question, because we spend upwards of $18 million per year on capital projects, including machinery. And as you said, much of it—including practically all our knitting machines—now comes from outside the country.

I think the US textile equipment industry has failed to put enough money into research and development in the past couple of decades. As a result, their products haven't been efficient enough. And several countries, the Swiss in particular, have moved in to capitalize on the vacuum.

Why have the Swiss been able to do what American industry has not?

There's been a lack of perception here. Meanwhile, the Swiss have had to be perceptive, because the country is so damn small in terms of population and geography that their industry has to prosper abroad in order to exist at all. Their whole history has been as a world producer and trader. And as a result, they've developed a great data bank and become extremely sensitive to what is happening all over the world. Their exposure to opportunity was enormous, in other words, and they saw it and seized it. Sweden's done the same thing.

How much of US industry's problem has been lack of perception? And how much of it has been due to an inability to accumulate capital because of taxation, financial policies or whatever?

I have to believe that taxation has not been the problem.

Let me give you the flip side of the Swiss thing. Until about twenty years ago, you could only buy watches with a jewel lever movement. To make that movement required long apprenticeships to train highly skilled workers.

Along comes Timex and says, "Hell, let's make it with a pin lever. We'll sell it at a low price and, if it only lasts a year or two, the buyer can throw it away and still get a value." So there was a reverse case where a Swiss industry was literally wiped out. Because an American business utilized a technology whose significance didn't become apparent to the Swiss until it was too late.

You're saying that perception, or the lack of it, is what counts?

Right. I don't believe it's the lack of capital that's hurt US industry, but rather a lack of perception about what's happening in the environment. If a company is alert, imaginative, aggressive and oriented toward research and development, it's going to make strides.

In this context, what companies do you particularly admire?

Well, Eastman Kodak, which has done an incredible job with film. I think Minnesota Mining has been very imaginative. Johnson and Johnson in the medical consumer products field. IBM is certainly an outstanding example. And I'd have to mention American Home Products Corporation. And Beatrice Foods of Chicago has shown phenomenal growth.

You don't have to mention company names, but what industries do you feel have been unresponsive, unperceptive?

Oh, I think a hell of a lot of them have been derelict in the sense. Look at what Japan has done to our electronics industries, to the camera business and so forth.

US auto makers haven't been very perceptive, either. For a long time, two companies "owned" the automobile business in this country, and I think they felt they could overpower any competition. They had an enormous sense of security about their huge shares of the market. And I think if they'd been less of a monopoly, they never would have permitted the encroachment by foreign firms. But they felt impervious.

Do any other industries come to mind?

Well, banks have in one sense been overly expansive, I think. They want to create holding companies and move into overseas and real estate investments and all that at once. They're failing to mind the store and to maintain the quality of the business they know best, which is making loans to people and to companies. They've stopped doing their homework on the businesses they own.

What makes you think that?

Well, for instance, I sat with the heads of several banks that had a $350 million stake in W.T. Grant's. I told them that it takes a long time to turn a retail operation around—as long as it took for it to turn sour. I said that Grant's should either be abandoned or be given a minimum of six or seven years and all the money it needs. From my experience in Milwaukee, I know you can't just take a retail operation and say, "Make it well." It takes years of work and all the energy, intelligence and imagination you can muster, plus a stout heart and a long purse.

But the banks didn't realize that soon enough with Grant's?

Right. You know, they may still have a lot of loans in their portfolios from companies that should be in bankruptcy. But they don't want to recognize the problems. If they did, they'd have to take an enormous markdown and publicly announce their stupidity. So they keep thinking they'll pull themselves out of the hole.

Do you think that if the banks had been more perceptive, some of those loans might never have been made in the first place?

Well, I couldn't say for sure. I can only emphasize how important I think it is for a chief executive to understand the changing environment and how it impacts on his business. It isn't an easy task, particularly because, to really gain perspective on important social, economic and political issues, you have to be able to step back from the business and view them objectively.

Could you sum the way you see your job, Pete, in terms of looking at the broad environment?

Well, I think we make a series of environmental assumptions whenever we're formulating long-range corporate plans. We take data that's already available, that's ground out by the ton by government and other agencies. And we distill it to get at the substantive data that we think could affect our universe of opportunities and industries.

We look at textiles on a worldwide basis, for example, and ask ourselves such questions as, "Will the industry eventually gravitate largely to low-cost labor countries? Particularly in the segments of our business where labor accounts for a large percentage of cost, that trend has already begun. It's happening in South Korea, Hong Kong, Formosa, India, and the Philippines.

Is Springs Mills involved in any of this?

Somewhat, but we've found that we don't have the stomach for it. The Japanese are doing much more of it. They had a highly successful textile industry going in their own country. But inflation and energy costs finally drove their costs to a point where they could no longer compete in many areas. So they exported their capital and technology to low-cost labor countries.

Singapore? Korea?

Yes, you name it. So I ask myself, "Will that trend continue?" Will more and more of the industry move to low-cost labor countries? And will it next be the third world—China, the African nations—that gives us the real competition?

You tell me.
I think there's a high probability that, as those underdeveloped countries raise their living standards, they will start to attract these kinds of universal industries with high labor costs. More and more finished articles would then come into this country, which would cut into our share of the market.

So that's a good example of the sort of environmental trend we have to look at. We have to ask ourselves whether we're really going to stem imports and whether we really desire to do that. Or are we going to say, "Hey, the cheapest way to help a developing nation is to buy their merchandise and to support, maybe even invest in, their own newer industries."

I get the feeling that you think it will be the latter, rather than a ban on imports.
Yes, I do think imports will continue to grow here. And, as I've said, we have to take that into consideration in our strategies for future directions.

What other environmental trends might figure in Springs' future?
Well, we're looking at OSHA and the requirements we have in our industry concerning noise level, cotton dust lung disease and so on. And we have to consider the billions it will cost us to conform and the effect that that expense will have on our cash flow and energy needs.

We also have to consider, for instance, the effect of new industry moving into our areas with much higher entry-level wages. Michelin Tires, for example, starts people at $4 an hour. Our average wage is lower than that.

So there you have a few examples of the kinds of things we take into account in the course of intermediate and long-range planning. It requires an enormous amount of time to sense which environmental factors will have a significant plus or minus impact on our industry. And then you have to redirect the enterprise's capital so as to minimize your risk. Even when you do a good job, it's a hell of a gamble.

Ralph E. BeVard

President and Chief Executive Officer
Eraser Company, Inc.

In a world of huge corporations, numerous small companies continue to demonstrate that the small-time entrepreneur can still find a niche to fill.

The Eraser Company, a Syracuse, New York firm that employs only fifty people, offers a case in point. Founded in 1911 to manufacture erasers, the firm has survived for well over half a century by building a reputation of quality and by expanding into product lines that would be impractical for larger companies to tackle.

Ralph E. BeVard joined Eraser's board of directors in 1958, while he was operating a family-owned machine shop. Two years later, when the president of Eraser resigned, BeVard agreed to take over the top spot "temporarily." The firm, which had then been floundering, suddenly began to again show a profit under his leadership, and BeVard became president on a permanent basis. Over the years, he bought controlling stock from some fifty other shareholders.

Since then, annual sales have jumped about 800 percent to the present $1.5 million figure. The company continues to manufacture fiberglass erasers, but wire-stripping machinery, which joined its product line in the late 1940s, now accounts for approximately 90 percent of sales. Having bought out several smaller firms in recent years, Eraser today also manufactures and sells such other industrial specialty items as component lead-forming equipment for printed circuit boards.

Mr. BeVard is a past president of the Syracuse Junior Chamber of Commerce and an advisor to the US Small Business Administration.

How do your problems differ from those of a billion-dollar company, Ralph?

Well, I don't think a small business necessarily has any more or fewer problems than a large one. But the problems are unique and of a different magnitude.

When a small business is just getting started, the person at the top has to be a salesman, engineer, financier, personnel man and all the other functions. That's fine, because he learns a lot about all these functions as the business grows. But there comes a time when one or more of these functions needs expansion and more specialized attention than the owner can afford to give. That's when it becomes difficult. You're not used to hiring people for these specialties, and you've got to pick the right ones. Not having this kind of experience, it was necessary to acquire the knowledge of how to choose people.

When did you yourself reach the point where you needed to hire specialists?

About four or five years ago, our customer feedback showed us that there were many products not already in our line that were needed in the marketplace. Customers would send samples of wires that they wanted stripped, and we'd encounter problems our machines couldn't handle. We needed new machines, but we had to develop them from scratch and I personally just didn't have the time.

You needed to bring in a specialist for that job?

We needed more than one. It's very difficult to find one person who can conceive the ideas and mechanical principles and also can design and engineer the products. If we hired one person, he'd need supporting services that we didn't have. It was a real problem. Finally I found the right man.

How did you persuade him to come to your company?

I simply offered him the job and the challenge. In our area, many operations have been phased out of large firms. Literally thousands of good people have been returned to the labor market. So we can easily get people of high calibre.

He felt that his present job was in danger?

Yes, he happened to be a member of our church, and the minister had also mentioned him to me. But we always have a large quantity of resumes from this type personnel. The talent is available.

Ralph E. BeVard

Ralph, tell me about this specialist you hired. How did he adjust to the move from a large company to a small one?

Well, he told me recently that this has been a new experience for him. He's had to become a kind of business manager in his area. He's had to become more resourceful, to use more of his native talents in order to become more valuable to himself and to the company.

For instance?

I'd come in in the morning, and he'd say, "Where is my drafting help?" At his former firm, when something was outside the realm of his capabilities, he'd simply go into the office next door, and get the help he needed. We just didn't have those resources. He had a lot of adjusting to do in this respect.

Hiring him must have been a critical turning point for you. I assume he couldn't pay for himself right away, and I wonder how you felt when you took the gamble on him.

A salary of his magnitude on the payroll is significant in the overall financial picture of a company of our size.

One alternative was to subcontract on a job basis. Another was to hire moonlighters, which is what we'd done in the past. But I decided to gamble, to hire more people than we needed at the time. It hasn't totally paid off yet, but we now have a significant engineering facility which is functioning well.

At first, though, you used moonlighters?

Yes. I had one man who came in at night for about twenty years, since even before I had joined the company. We then hired another moonlighter about ten years ago, and he's still working with us.

How have those arrangements worked out?

You do have added communications problems with the moonlighters, because they come in at night. You're not there when they are; you have to just take them at their word and see their work in the results. With the help of notes and the phone, on the other hand, you can get something done. When you're not there personally to supervise, you have to be careful to keep his work from getting routine.

After a while, though, you began to hire full-time specialists?

Yes, we hired the first one a couple of years ago. A very good engineer from a national electronics firm. I was a little bit scared. I never would have gotten into it if it could have endangered the financial situation of the company, but I still worried about injecting something into the system that wasn't immediately paying off. I knew I was taking a chance.

But it's worked out?

Very well. We've kept a list of about 40 products that we needed to develop and we're crossing them off one by one. We're getting them into production.

Did this man start with you at salary comparable to what he'd made at his former company?

No. On many jobs, there isn't too much difference between our salaries and those paid by the bigger companies, but generally we can't afford to give our people quite as much. Of course, we have many good benefits. Profit-sharing and pension plans, an excellent vacation plan and so on.

The law of supply and demand operates in Syracuse just like anywhere else. If a large company has a contract they have to get through, wages mean nothing to them. If they need toolmakers, and the going rate is $5 an hour, they'll go out and offer a toolmaker $7 an hour.

Well, there comes a time when the contract is completed. Then these fellows that have been making $7 an hour are again in the market. It becomes a very difficult situation for them. They've attuned themselves to this income. Now they have to go back to $5 or $5.50 an hour. We simply can't match some of those rates.

Still, why don't your employees take the first opportunity to leave you for a bigger company and a higher wage?

Well, we do have some turnover, but the rate is decreasing. I think the recessions of recent years have made people less transient. But the rest of the answer is that there are some people who just prefer to work for a small company.

There's a human touch. I'll give you an example. We've always held a Christmas party for our people. But last year, for the first time, we took them out to a clambake. I didn't think it turned out too well. So this year I decided, "Well, we won't have a clambake."

Then, just about a month ago, one of our employees came to me and said that one of the people had been with us for 15 years and we ought to have a clambake to celebrate. I didn't think that was a good enough reason, but I got the message. They *wanted* a clambake. So last Saturday, we all went to a clambake.

You can consider their wishes without a whole layer of corporate bureaucracy?
Certainly. If one of our employees has a problem, he can come directly in here and talk to me. I know them all personally.

What kinds of problems might they bring you?
Well, usually at tax time, there's always at least one who needs an advance of a couple hundred dollars.

Do you provide it?
Oh, yes, I don't think we've ever refused.

Psychologically, Ralph, people appreciate it when the boss takes care of them in ways like that. At the same time, though, they tend to resent being dependent. Do you sense this from your experience?
Yes. They want help, but not too much of it. You know, we all need assistance from other people, but you have to be careful not to go too far with it.

From what I hear, you've done a lot to help people, and not just within the company. I'd like to talk a bit about your involvement in community affairs.
One of the best things I ever did was to become a member, many years ago, of the Syracuse Junior Chamber of Commerce. That gave me an opportunity to get leadership training for myself. I had a chance to head many committees and to work in many areas of civic concern. And it was a regular business operation; you know, we'd put committees together, come up with funding, see projects through. A great experience.
Well, of course, age gets you out of the Junior Chamber of Commerce. In more recent years, I've been active in the Manufacturers Association of Syracuse. We're also very involved, my wife and I, and the company, in the new Civic Center here. Down through the years, I've been connected with many, many other things, too. I worked with the Boy Scouts for a long

time, and was a Scout Master until I got married. I was president of the PTA, and so on.

What have you learned from these experiences?

That it's possible to get people to do things. At first, I'd be truly surprised when I'd call a list of people to solicit help on a project and so many would say, "Sure, sure."

Did you discover any differences between big corporations and smaller businesses in terms of their willingness to get involved?

No, except that the bigger corporations were generous in letting people out on company time, which is understandable. You know, this becomes a big thing to a small company.

It's often said, particularly by college students, that business doesn't give a damn about the community and is just interested in the quick buck. Do you ever hear that? And, having been so deeply involved in the community, how do you reply?

Well, I hear it, and it's a difficult problem to deal with. The businessman is continually being downgraded by society and the media.

I've known many businessmen all my life, and they're among the most compassionate people I've ever met. It's never difficult for me to call any businessman and ask him to do something that will help somebody where there's a real need.

For example, during the many years when I worked with the New York State Parole Board in Syracuse, I called on a lot of businessmen to try to help ex-cons find jobs. And I was never turned down. Never! And these businessmen are supposed to have no compassion for others!

They were always willing to take a chance on somebody?

Yes. One time, the president of a large corporation called me up and said a certain fellow had applied for a job and given my name. In this particular case, based on my experience, I was sure he wouldn't work out. I said, "I wouldn't hire him if I were you. He'll do you no good, and I don't think you can do him any good. He's been out of prison many times as a result of my efforts, only to finally end up back in." I did the best I could to unsell him on this man. But he hired him anyway, in a real, but misguided, desire to help.

This is a businessman who's not supposed to have compassion. In my opinion, it is unfortunate that businesses and businessmen are classed as "unfeeling and uncaring." It is simply not true.

What happened in that case, Ralph? Did the fellow work out?
No, he didn't, though we all hoped that he would.

How often, in your experience, does the ex-con succeed on the job?
Well, it's frustrating. I've helped fifty or one hundred to get jobs, but getting them to work out is something else. Maybe 50 percent wind up back in jail. We still do it for the sake of the ones who do succeed. One of the men I helped, for example, ultimately became chief quality control man for a very large corporation. This was a guy who'd been in for armed assault. One success of this type can make it all worthwhile.

Particularly since you're so involved in the community, Ralph, you must interact with a lot of people from the many large corporations here. What are the differences that hit you? Do you shake your head about what goes on at the big companies?
One of the big things I notice is that they lose the ability to stay close to events. You know, somebody will make a mistake and, by the time news of it gets passed up the line, it's too late to do anything about it.

In a big company, also, they tend to take the desires and needs of top echelon people for granted until they're faced with resignations or union demands from the production workers. They begin to treat people as part of a mechanical corporate system, rather than as people. I know it's difficult. If the Eraser Company became a big corporation tomorrow, I'd probably find myself headed in the same direction.

What other differences have you noted?
Well, I understand that the large companies didn't become large by spending money foolishly. But I know I have to be a lot more meticulous than they when I say we're going to spend $5,000 on something.

Also, because large businesses usually tend toward volume, they lose their perspective. For instance, one company can only make soup, and that's a very narrow thing.

Why is it any more narrow than making wire-stripping machines?
Because we have seventy-five completely different products in our line. They may have twenty-five or thirty soups, but they're all in the same

cans and they all go through basically the same manufacturing process. Each of our products requires a different process.

I'll tell you another difference between big business and the situation here. Big business doesn't worry about perpetuating their operations. The future is paved. But in the small company, there aren't sufficient ranks from which to draw people who can run things smoothly. So who's going to carry on? Your children? In some cases, maybe with the fortunes of fifty people at stake.

What's going to happen to this business when you retire?

I really don't know at this point. But I'm 61 and, though I have no present plans to retire, I am trying to take steps now to see that the company is perpetuated.

Have you thought about selling the business? Have any large corporations offered to buy you out?

Oh, we've had a number of offers. We don't plan to sell, but we'll always talk to people because you never can tell. You know, everything's for sale at the right price.

Why do you think a large firm would be interested in buying the Eraser Company?

Because we're highly profitable and well-known. We have an excellent reputation throughout the world.

One reason for that, I think, is that we absolutely do not argue with a customer if he says he's not satisfied. Our guarantees have no time limits. And if someone who bought a machine from us ten years ago isn't happy with it, all he has to do is send it back and we'll refund the full purchase price. No questions asked.

Has that happened often?

No, quite seldom. But it has happened. I once met a fellow from RCA who said he'd had one of our machines for six years and it hadn't worked properly, so he had never used it. I said, "Send it back." He said, "No, it was six years ago." This fellow couldn't believe this. And the next day, he brought by a few of his associates and they proceeded to buy some more of our equipment.

The industry knows we operate this way. They know they don't have to worry when they deal with us. And I think that gives us an edge on the competition.

Do you have much competition?

Our main competitor is here in the Syracuse area. It's a firm that was started by a man who was with the Eraser Company back in the late 1940s, when we were just getting into our wire-stripping equipment lines.

Do you keep a close watch on that company's prices?

Oh, yes. We watch all competitors' pricing. And, of course, we have to keep them in mind when we set a price on a job.

Do any big companies compete with you on any of your lines?

Yes. There's a firm in Illinois, for instance. But the larger companies don't really hurt us, because there isn't enough volume in our type of equipment for them to spend a lot of time and money pushing it. With them, it's just a convenience item. Another thing to offer people who are already their customers.

People say that big businesses are squeezing out little ones, but here's an example of a little company meeting needs better than the big ones can. Am I right?

Well, everyday we open the mail and there's a big company asking us to do something they can't do economically.

Like what?

Stripping wires. It's something they need us for and there's not much they can do about it—short of investing more money in the problem than it would be worth to them.

So you've found a niche and it's worked for you. But the Eraser Company is sixty-five years old, and some people would say that those sorts of opportunities don't exist anymore. Do you think there are niches to be filled by new small business today?

I don't think there's any question about it. The opportunity in small business is still there. The problem is that, in general, people today are ill-prepared to get into it. They've never had the inclination to apply themselves to the task.

Why not?

What do you hear about every student today? "You're capable of doing much more than you're doing." And therein lies the problem, I think.

People don't realize their capabilities. We're not any smarter than kids today. It's just a matter of how we use what we have.

But why do you think young people are underachieving? And why do you think they're not going into business?

For one thing, the educational system doesn't provide for it; it's not in the curriculum. They provide for engineers, doctors, lawyers, but they don't specifically prepare people to go into business for themselves. And I think that's a big thing, because students aren't really conscious of the fact that they could do it. Even aside from the educational factor, people just don't see how they can fill a need in business. But they can, and it generally doesn't even take a lot of capital to get started.

Of course, it helps if Daddy already owns the business.

Not necessarily. I know two businesses in town that the father had run for many years. He thought that no one could help but love his son, "because he's my son. How could anyone dislike him?"

So he brought in his son to run the business. And of course, the older people who had been there for many years disliked the son. It was just natural. But the father paid no attention to this. So the next thing you know, he had a union on his hands. The son had antagonized the employees just by being there. He had come between the employees and his father. They didn't like it.

You have eight children. Have any of them expressed going into business for themselves?

No. I think they look on it as being too difficult. The older ones have seen what I've gone through to get where I am. And I think they may wonder if it isn't too high a price to pay.

What do they see? Long hours of work?

Yes, long hours of work and being away from home. This is in the past now, those years of not having enough money and struggling to meet the payroll.

They've seen the problems, but somehow haven't sensed the pleasure you've gotten out of it?

Well, my oldest daughter is forty-one now, and the older ones have gone off on their own. And it's hard for them, being of a different generation, to go through the same steps I did.

But you think it's been worth it. The pleasures outweigh the problems you've had?

Of course. You know, I think operating a business is one of the best things anyone can do. It's challenging, rewarding and romantic. Next to God and my family, this is the most important thing in my life. And I'm not the only person who feels this way. Once someone has gone into business for himself, you can hardly ever get him to be an employee again. Once he's had a taste of it, that's all he wants, regardless of how badly he's fared. Business is like life itself. It's fraught with many problems. Solving these problems is the result of hard work, dedication, and determination to succeed.

You used the word "romantic" a moment ago. Wire-stripping? Romantic?

I think there's romance in anything we set out to do and then do right. If somebody wants to learn how to play the piano and succeeds, the rewards are of the romantic type. Maybe it's not quite the right word, but that's basically what I feel.

I know what you mean, but a cynic is going to say, "You mean, you see romance in a wire-stripping machine?"

What can I say? Just in the area of competition, there's so much romanticism that it isn't funny. Anybody who tries to downgrade competition in business is making a horrible mistake. It's one of the greatest things in the world. And I've always said that if you take care of the business, it will take care of you.

Despite the lure of competition, have you ever drawn the line on growth and said to yourself, "I love it just the way it is. It's comfortable and it's giving me a good living"? Or do you keep pushing for more growth?

You have to keep pushing to grow. That's what makes it romantic.

Thomas H. Wyman

President and Chief Executive Officer
Green Giant Company

It's quite a feat to sell more than $425,000,000 worth of peas and corn and other food products and services each year, and to make the Green Giant name synonymous with the finest quality. Skillful marketing, brilliant advertising, and superb production methods, including the development of special hybrid seeds, are responsible.

Green Giant is an old, established company, founded in Le Sueur, Minnesota, in what is now known as "The Valley of the Jolly Green Giant." Today, its operations are worldwide.

Early in 1975, its Board elected a new president and chief executive officer, 46-year old Thomas H. Wyman, a native of St. Louis, Missouri. He was a 1951 graduate, *magna cum laude*, of Amherst College. At the time of his election to the Green Giant Company presidency, Mr. Wyman was senior vice president, general manager, and chairman of the management executive committee of Polaroid Corporation.

Tom, you're the prototype of the professional manager. You left a job where you ran an advanced technology company and took over a company that cans peas and corn. Quite a change. Is your job totally different?

Before I joined Polaroid I had spent ten years with the Nestle Company—so I knew something about the food industry. But over the last ten years I was with Polaroid and in many ways the worlds of Polaroid and Green Giant are quite different.

It's said that a really skilled top professional manager can move without trouble from one industry to another. But is it really that easy?

I don't think there's anything very difficult about it. You've got to recognize that every company has an atmosphere and operating format of its own. If an experienced manager with reasonable sensitivity invests the time to understand the new company's products, markets, and organization, he should be successful.

Still, you're the first person ever to go directly to the presidency of Green Giant without having come up through the ranks.

Yes, and I think there are disadvantages and advantages to that. Someone who comes up through the ranks has already proven himself within the company by the time he gets to the top. He's built up working relationships through the years. He knows to whom to turn for key assignments. On the other hand, someone from the outside may find it easier to introduce changes. The outsider will take less as given and he will ask more questions.

At Polaroid, Tom, you had a lot of power and responsibility. Why did you move to Green Giant?

There's a difference between being near the top of a company and having the chance to run it. I'm not saying that it was an easy decision. I was very happy at Polaroid, but it wasn't at all clear when additional operating responsibility might develop. The Green Giant opportunity came up quite unexpectedly and I decided I should accept it. Chances like this one don't come up often.

Aside from the job itself, what attracted you to Green Giant?

When they approached me, I looked very carefully at their record. I think it's a special kind of company. It was clear to me that for many years they have been doing what most companies continually try to do: to turn out a better product than the competitors. I was fascinated by the opportunities represented by the unique Green Giant image and by the strength of their market position.

When the board gave the word you had the job, Tom, how did you prepare to take over?

I guess I just took several deep breaths. You don't have the time to do any specific preparation. You go to the airport.

When you arrived here, what were the first things you did?

On my first day here we had a meeting with all the department managers in Le Sueur—in the basement of the Methodist Church. That's the biggest meeting place in town. I guess there were 300 people in attendance. And the following Monday, we had another meeting with fifty or sixty people here in our new headquarters in Chaska.

In both meetings, I talked a bit about the way I saw my role here. I tried to talk in a general way about why I was excited about coming to Green Giant and about the prospects for the future. I emphasized building on the past, rather than threatening major changes.

What reaction did you get?

I guess I'd be the last to know what was said after the meetings. But, generally speaking, I think the reaction was, "So far, so good. He certainly seems serious—doesn't know much about corn and peas, but maybe he's teachable. Let's wait and see."

Since those meetings, what have you done to let people know what you expect from them?

I believe that every manager has a responsibility to communicate regularly with those he supervises to agree as accurately as possible on what is expected and to evaluate their performance. I've done a lot of that. Also, when I first came here I formed a management committee which has become the key instrument in running the company.

And did the message about regular performance evaluation get across?

Unfortunately, no. About four months later, I asked for a thermometer reading and found that only about 20 percent of the people had been performance rated.

How did that make you feel?

I wasn't left with a sense of power and influence. We talked about it some more, but after another couple of months there was still considerable inertia and resistance. Everyone was professing the faith, but nothing happened.

How did you finally handle the situation?

I finally had to draw the line and just say, "Now do it." I indicated that in order for merit increase recommendations to be reviewed, a manager would have to have a fully current record on evaluating the people reporting to him. And, not surprisingly, the picture changed immediately.

Just like that. When their compensation was tied to it.

Yes. That finally got the point across that we were interested in living differently.

What do you mean, "living differently?"

The Green Giant culture has been somewhat relaxed, at least in comparison to the business world in which I had been living. We're trying to adjust that a little bit. Take working hours. Our office opens at 8 o'clock in the morning and closes at 4:30.

Three years ago there were very few people in the headquarters who did not leave promptly at 4:30. There was not much of a sense of urgency in some areas. What wasn't completed today could be done tomorrow or the day after. I believe we are living somewhat differently now.

How did you get them to "live differently?"

It's not very complicated. If you call a couple of meetings at 4 o'clock (which will obviously last for an hour or two), that begins to communicate a message. Or you leave a note on someone's desk at 5 o'clock saying you're sorry they couldn't meet with you. You follow up the next day on requests for information. You suggest close-in deadlines. You answer your own mail very promptly.

Tom, how did you prepare yourself for those first moves? Where did you turn to start learning the company?

You start with the written material—the policy manuals, the strategy, the operating plans, and the financial data. But this is just a start. How do you find out about the people and how they work? What is the general atmosphere? How do the managers and supervisors see their jobs? The answers to these questions are not in the files. It's like moving into a new neighborhood. You have to figure out who's on the street, who's important, who's interesting, who makes things happen. And that takes a certain amount of time.

How long? A year?

Probably less. You start off with a high resolve to be very careful and thoughtful—slow to reach conclusions. But if you're a manager, you can't resist the process where judgments form themselves. And confronted with your judgments, you must act. It's an unconscious process, I think, over which we don't have very much control.

How were you received by the officers of this company, who suddenly found themselves with a new boss from the outside? Inevitably, some of them must have been worried about their jobs.

I suppose there was some anxiety. It was clear to most that some organizational changes would—and should—be made. This has happened, but I believe that the process has been reasonably smooth.

The reaction I didn't want was: "We're on Dunkirk Beach—are we landing or evacuating?" I wanted a sense of rational analysis and fairness to come across. I also wanted a sense of action, direction, and decisiveness. I wanted to get past the reflexive apprehension, to take time for the management group to understand each other and to share information and problems. And I wanted to find out where we had leverage so we could make changes where they mattered.

And not just arbitrarily.

Right. When people see that you're acting thoughtfully, and not impulsively, there's a massive sigh of relief that says, "We may have been drifting somewhat but now we're going to get organized." Letting people go or dropping product lines is a tough business. But you do the best you can. If we're going to compete successfully in the industry, there's no way around it.

How have people reacted?

In my view, very well. I am so convinced that people recognize it when performance (theirs or their associates') isn't up to the demands of the situation. When a good performer sees another man getting away with poor performance, he figures, "Why bother? It doesn't make any difference what I do." In the end, I think, getting rid of dead weight is, paradoxically, a quick way to improve morale. Then people know that good performance is recognized. They like it.

You've made a good number of personnel changes.

Yes, there have been a number of moves at the management level.

In what areas have you made the most changes?

One of the areas where we have worked intensively has been the financial area. I saw a need to elevate the level of involvement and skill of the financial people throughout the company. You cannot make sound decisions without accurate data. And it is so important that the data has meaning for the people working with it—that it *lives*.

They were just score-keepers.

Right. If an accountant reports, for example, that we lost $80,000, he must have a sense of being part of the team that lost it. He can't just report the figures and blame them on poor production or poor sales or whatever. I wanted some help, some solutions, some involvement; not just a report on success or failure.

When you got deeper into the company, did you identify some men as particularly capable?

Yes. We have brought in only a few people from outside the company. Most of our needs were met by people already here.

What made people stand out as exceptional?

I appreciate very much the people who understand the intimate detail of their operations but have a clear perspective of the whole. I like people who are organized and have a feel for what matters. I confess to liking people who work hard—conspicuously and effectively—and set a tone for their people. I like the people who know their people well.

Did some managers try to ingratiate themselves with you by flattery or by telling you what they thought you wanted to hear?

I suppose so. I've had to cut off one or two apparent overtures of that sort. But I don't get too much of it. I think I'm seen as being far more responsive to performance—the merits of a case—than to a more emotional or social approach. And I think that people have come to know what I expect in terms of performance.

Was morale low when you arrived here?

It wasn't too high. It was a healthy atmosphere in most senses, but I think there was a sense of unfulfilled potential. The situation wasn't helped by the fact that an early frost had seriously limited the corn crop the previous summer. There was also some visible cause for anxiety with respect to the company's balance sheet.

How did you decide what needed to be done to turn the situation around?

I've come to appreciate what I used to think was an overly serious and religious attention to numbers. I was interested, first of all, in a meaningful financial analysis. I wanted to pinpoint the significant numbers and lay out a sort of numerical road map to keep us on the track.

They hadn't done this before you arrived?

There were plans, of course, but they were somewhat informal and the monitoring of progress against objectives was not tight.

Why do you suppose this was so?

I don't think it was so surprising. The company had grown well through the years. I had seen a somewhat similar pattern at Polaroid in the mid-1960s.

It happens when you have too much success; too rapid a growth rate, where time is more important than money. You begin throwing resources at problems. You develop layers of people. You develop services that are interesting but, in the aggregate, too expensive. Everybody begins to play adult monopoly all over the place and overheads and costs move rapidly out of proportion to reality and good business.

And you saw a similar situation at Green Giant?

Right. The business was growing with a certain inertia. There was time for moss to grow without being disturbed. Facilities were open which might have been closed long ago. This happens if you have not been serious and rigorous in your performance evaluation. You need constant pruning of the trees.

Whereas one of my first reactions here was dismay, it was a dismay mixed with excitement. I thought it should be possible to manage the business better—at all levels—and that if we could, the payoff in improved results could be very great.

When they see the new man means business, they get the message. It is important that people feel that you're making the changes that really matter and not just stirring up the waters.

To that end, what actions have you taken?

One of the first things I noticed was that the company had a tendency to try to do too many things at once. There were too many projects in the works to be really effective with most of them. When I arrived, Green Giant was working on 116 new products, and it was confusing. We set up a New Products Committee to examine those projects and the development focus was centered on about 25 of them in the first year.

What else have you done?

I decided that Green Giant has great potential in overseas markets, so we're working to build up our international activity. We have also put the company in better financial condition by reducing costs and improving inventory controls. This was a pressing need.

Coming to Green Giant, you had to acclimate yourself to more than a different business environment. You moved from the sophisticated culture of Boston to a smaller midwestern community.

What is really different about this part of the world—and it's very interesting to be a part of it—is the business community's sense of itself, of its own identity.

What do you mean, Tom?

It's kind of a prosaic example, but in Boston, getting a capable executive to manage the United Way campaign is not easy. In the East, the attitude is, "Who can we get to handle this for us?" Whereas here it's just sort of assumed that supporting the United Way is part of a chief executive's job. We have a long list of major corporations here in the Minneapolis and St. Paul area and the chief executives take their civic responsibilities very seriously.

Business people are more committed to their communities here?

Yes, I think the business community here has a strong sense of its identity and of its responsibilities. When a company appoints a new president or chairman here it is a common practice to have a reception for him. All of the key business leaders show up for these occasions. It's a nice idea that fifty or sixty heads of companies will make such an effort. The reason people attend those functions is not because they think they should; they really want to, and when they get there they know everybody. In Boston, the Raytheons, the Gillettes, the Polaroids know each other, of course, but in a different way. There is not a comparable sense of common purpose because there are not as many common causes.

And they accepted you right away in the Twin Cities?

In the first place, you're exposed to people very rapidly here—that's the way it works. There's a tremendous openness and pride in the region and in the role the major companies have played in making the Twin Cities such a special place. They really care about the area and they want to be sure that you do, too.

Shortly after you came to Green Giant you gave quite a talk about corporate social responsibility. You asked how many business leaders expressed their reactions personally to the heads of corporations who were involved in illegal political gifts, payoffs, pollution, and the like. You questioned what you called the ill-conceived code that it's inappropriate for one corporate executive to question another's business ethics.

I was suggesting to the Rotary Club that we have failed to monitor our own business world. How rigorous have we been with each other? We've left the policing of business to angry students and housewives.

But now a lot of people are trying to tell us we're wrong. The outside world is wary of the poetry we have composed for our annual reports.

We must do much better in living up to our responsibilities—corporate leaders in particular. We ought to be able to meet our social responsibilities and set ethical standards for ourselves and for each other better than others can set them for us. In fact, if we really believe in free enterprise then we can't afford not to do this. I guess this was the substance of my speech.

How did the business community react?

In general, very positively. At least I heard nothing from people who disagreed. I had a number of supportive responses from business leaders, but also from housewives and young people. A number of middle managers were apparently quite pleased though. They were saying, "My faith in the system is really restored," and, "I didn't know anybody would be willing to get that far out on a limb," and, "I hope my boss read that speech."

You named names; you were very specific. It was one of the most impressive talks I've read in years. Did you get any negative reaction from other chief executives?

No. I did get a call from the public relations department of an out-of-town company. They'd heard about the speech and wanted a copy. I couldn't resist asking what they thought of it. And the response was, "Oh, I'm not allowed to say. We haven't formulated our reaction yet." But, in general, the winds have changed and people are with us. Some respond a little more constructively than others. But everybody knows that corporate social responsibility is something we must be talking about and doing something about.

To sum up, Tom, let's say that a friend of yours was about to go from one corporation to a chief executive's post at another company. Based on your experience in the past fifteen months, what advice could you give him?

I'd tell him to beware of letting people believe that problems can be solved by some magic. It takes time to make changes—and it should. It's never going to go precisely as you might wish it to. It's not a very original thought, but virtually everything depends on ensuring that the right people are in the right jobs with an ability to work well together.

It also takes time to be sure that you've sorted out the tasks and put the right ones up front. Maybe I'm a little sensitive about this because when I came here the expectation level was very high. I guess I've worried about not delivering results as rapidly as I wished or the miracles that some may have hoped for.

Thomas H. Wyman

95

Well, there aren't any miracles.
I know. I've discovered that.

Louis T. Hagopian

*Chairman of the Board
and Chief Executive Officer*
NW Ayer ABH International

NW Ayer is America's oldest advertising agency. It was founded in 1869 by Francis Wayland Ayer, then age twenty-one. Young Ayer, believing that businessmen might resent dealing with a youngster, named the new agency after his father, calling it NW Ayer & Son. Ayer has developed a reputation as one of advertising's foremost pioneers.

Ayer was the first advertising firm to hire a full-time copywriter (1892); to undertake a market research study (1897); to establish a public relations department (1919); to broadcast a radio commercial (1922) and to produce a commercial TV program (1946).

In 1976, annual billings exceeded the $200 million mark (more, if you count joint ventures undertaken by Ayer's international wing). Its billings have more than doubled since 1967. Of the nation's top twenty agencies, only two have grown at a faster rate over the past decade than Ayer has.

Among its clients, many of whom have been with the firm for years, Ayer counts DuPont, General Motors and the US Army. AT&T has been Ayer's client since 1908. That's one of the oldest client-agency relationships in advertising.

Louis T. Hagopian came to Ayer in 1960 after twelve years with General Motors and Chrysler Corporation in sales promotion and advertising posts. He was Director of Advertising and Sales Promotion for Chrysler's Plymouth Division before joining Ayer in Detroit as account supervisor on the Plymouth automobile account.

Mr. Hagopian was elected a Vice President of Ayer after two years, Executive Vice President and General Manager of the New York office after seven years, Vice Chairman of the Board after 13 years, and Chairman in 1976. After more than a century, he's only the sixth person to head the agency.

Lou, there's an old cliche that all the assets in a service business go down the elevator every night at five o'clock. That applies pretty well to Ayer, doesn't it?

Yes it does. A manufacturing company doing our volume of business would have to invest many millions of dollars in capital. But with the exception of the $3 million we've got tied up in furniture, fixtures, audio-visual equipment, plus enough working capital to carry our receivables, all we have is people. We've got a little over 900 people, very special people. Salaries account for about 70 percent of our costs.

Capital isn't that important?

You don't need much of an investment in plant and equipment. So anybody can get into the advertising agency business. It's a low investment situation, low entry fee.

That's why so many people start advertising agencies. Many of them have prospered in the business, working for somebody else. They leave to start their own firm, like Young and Rubicam. At one time those two men were working for Ayer in our Philadelphia office. What did they need to start? Just a place to put a typewriter, and a sign, some dreams and a lot of entrepreneurial spirit.

So you've got to handle your people carefully so they don't want to leave?

Well, I once remarked that if I ever got out of this business, I might be able to manage a professional sports team.

What's the analogy?

My job is to manage those people, those players, to keep an eye on their performance and pull them together.

It's not easy. If you're running an industrial company, there are a lot of quantitative areas, like manufacturing and engineering, where you can really put digits on things. Here you judge people and their productivity.

And you do more than judge them. Let's take that sports analogy another step. A major function of the manager is to communicate to the team the excitement that comes with knowing you're good at what you do, the excitement of being a winner.

Casey Stengel and Vince Lombardi knew a lot about their games, but what they did best was to make good players really want to win. And in our place, once you get over those crises of self-doubt that seem to affect people in service businesses, you work to instill a sense of confidence in these people, a lot of whom are real stars.

In advertising, we've been around for a long time, nearly 108 years, long enough to know that what we try will work and that the ideas we sell are good ones. We can have the assurance of knowing that we make things work.

We do change images, move products, affect the economy. This makes ours an exciting business. With the excitement of doing this comes the ability to accept the credit for a job well done and the ability to give credit to other people for the work they do. And out of that comes more excitement and even better work. That's what I believe and I try to get across to the people at the agency.

Here you have not ordinary people, but very, very creative people. How do you develop them?

You start by hiring the kind of bright people who tend to get involved. You don't want to have to needle people continually to get them to take the initiative and come up with ideas. The key word is involvement. Whatever your role in this business, the degree of involvement is very important.

So you find the people who will thrive on involvement, and then you try to create a climate where that attitude can flourish. You nurture it and encourage it by working to keep people interested.

How do you spot involved people?

In the agency they are the men and women who strive to understand the client's business, the kind of people who do more than take the standard factory tour and take the client to lunch. They go back and dig and study and learn. They visit the stores, learn the distribution problems, the personnel problems, the production problems. They care enough to get deeply into a client's business.

So you look for more than just good writers or conceptualizers when you select people. What are the clues you look for?

Obviously, you're looking for that thing called "desire." Motivation. Sometimes, it's raw and you can see it, feel it. Education is important, too, although I'm not hung up on the number of degrees or where they went to school. I want people who care, people who are innovators, regardless of where they went to school.

Advertising used to be regarded as a "blue blood" business. If you weren't an Easterner who went to Princeton . . . but that's changed, hasn't it? You're from the Midwest and you graduated from Michigan State, not the Ivy League. Yet, you made it to the top.

Well, when I joined the agency in Detroit, I didn't find too many "blue bloods" in the office. Not many of them were sent out there from Philadelphia. Because, with very few exceptions, the "blue bloods" didn't want to go out there and mix it up. The Brown boys, the Yale boys, the Princeton boys all seemed to stay East.

So I had no inferiority complex about not being an Ivy Leaguer or about the fact that my parents were immigrants. By the time I became really aware of the "blue bloods," I was being brought back East to become executive vice president of the company and general manager of the New York office.

The advertising business had already begun to change. How did the changes show?

In those old days, most selling was done at country clubs. They were playing the old school tie, the fraternity. The advertising agencies before the war simply reflected the way business was done in those days. That's the way it was. But it's changed now. The post-war period changed a lot of things.

In the late fifties and early sixties, more professional management came in. They had to perform. New managements realized they should take anybody who could help solve their problems. Today, client managements are accountable to stockholders in a much different way than they were in the old days. Stockholders and directors want managers who can produce higher earnings. They couldn't care less about their family and educational backgrounds.

Incidentally, in my travels abroad, I've discovered that the European countries haven't quite caught up with us yet in this regard. In some countries, the attitude still is, "I own this business. I'm going to turn it over to my son. You'll always be an employee."

They still face change abroad. But what about Ayer? Have you changed the way you handle employees?

Sure, just take a look at our business rules from the early days. We have a copy of our office regulations from 1877. Employees worked from 8 am to 6 pm. They got forty-five minutes for lunch—strictly enforced.

Let me read this one to you: "During business hours, loud talking, jesting, laughing or smoking will not be allowed, and the employees are particularly requested to avoid conversation with each other about any matters other than those strictly pertaining to the business of the firm." That's the way things were in those days.

You know, we're just a mirror of the American business scene. That, in turn, reflects the country as a whole. And it's all changed.

Your employees reflect the country, too. And there is certainly a strong anti-establishment feeling among many young people today. Since you hire so many creative people, I'm wondering whether you run into any of that. Good creative people who have those attitudes?

We've had people who, when we had cigarette business, refused to work on it. And as long as we had something else for them to do, we honored that. We had some people during the Vietnam war who didn't want to work on the Army account. Fortunately, that's not the case anymore since the All Volunteer Army. Our top people work on that account, which might explain why the advertising is outstanding and, more importantly, productive.

As aware and aggressive as advertising people can be, though, we've never had a problem where a bunch of people have demonstrated or walked in and made demands or anything like that. There hasn't been any of that kind of activism.

What about apathy? For example, have you ever hired a very able writer whose attitude, spoken or not, is, "My job is to write; I'm not interested in the client's business. You tell me the problem and I'll create the TV commercial."

No. A guy like that couldn't survive here or at the other good agencies. If he had such an attitude, we wouldn't hire him.

How often do you make a mistake in hiring?

Well, I believe if you bat somewhere over .500 in personnel selection, you're doing very well. You know, we've gone the whole route in this country, from the "just let me take a look at you" school to the very strict aptitude test. Those tests haven't worked out here. It's still an educated crap-shoot at best. Of course, you check the references and all that, but in the final analysis, you go with your instincts and you gamble. I'll tell you one of the biggest problems with young managers: They don't know when to go into the termination process. It's a tough thing for a young manager who hasn't done much hiring and firing to admit he made a mistake. He's afraid it will reflect badly on his performance.

So I've tried to reassure people here that, when it doesn't work out, both parties are better off if they face up to the mistake. I tell them: if someone comes here and it doesn't work out, you should say, "Look, we both made a mistake. Let's see if we can work this thing out so that neither of us suffers." In my judgment this is a lot more humane than letting these things drag out.

The ad industry has a reputation for very rapid turnover. Have you compared the turnover rate for professionals here with the rates in other industries?

Well, with us, the greatest turnover is with the people who've been with us the least amount of time and generally in the lower ranks.

At the higher levels, it's a different story. Of the fifty top people at this agency, for example, fifteen of us have never worked at another advertising agency.

That's stability. What characterizes the people who stay and advance here?

They're the ones who are most deeply involved, who have the most initiative. They care about a client's problems. His problems become theirs. They'll take initiatives with a client and not just react. If you look at the guys at the top of this business and how they've prospered, you'll have no doubt that they are the involved ones.

When a guy is really good, when he really gets into a client's problem, how do you prevent a situation where he becomes so indispensable that he starts making all kinds of demands?

You're touching on a very important part of this business which isn't discussed in public very often. We've got a lot of high-priced talent largely because this is such a high-risk business. So you can get a sort of Superstar situation.

A big question any agency chief executive has to face is this: how do I make sure that the client is relating to us as a total agency and not just to one individual?

Today, the advertising and marketing people at the client level are very astute people. They are a lot less affected by personal relationships with one agency person than they are concerned with the output and the involvement they get from the agency itself. Mostly, we're hired, reviewed and retained on the basis of sound, impersonal judgments. And we make it a point to see that our top management is as involved with the client's top management as our staff people are with his staff.

This brings up a whole other area. How do clients measure their satisfaction with an ad agency? I'm thinking back to a classic study on the effectiveness of advertising. The conclusion was that you can measure how many people were exposed to an ad and how many were influenced by it, but you can't measure its impact on sales. When the housewife gets to the supermarket, maybe she doesn't buy your product because the competitor's price or packaging is better. Or yours isn't on the shelf, or whatever. So the study concluded that you could only measure advertising as a medium of communication, not sales. If that's true, how do clients measure your effectiveness?

We try to agree with the client in advance on benchmarks that will determine the success of an ad campaign. Also, they're aware of the variables and limitations in advertising and how it relates to and ranks with other elements of marketing.

In the purchase of an automobile, for example, advertising ranks somewhere between numbers five and seven in marketing factors; previous experience, availability and quality of dealer service are some of the things that rate higher. Even with packaged goods, which is certainly the most advertising-intensive area, a lot of other factors are at work. Like product position, sampling, couponing, pricing, distribution and most importantly, product quality.

At Ayer, some years ago we developed a new product model, which takes all of the critical marketing factors into account. Using this model, we're able to predict with some accuracy what the advertising requirements will be and how effective both the advertising and, in fact, the entire product introduction will be. According to some of the people in the academic area, it's the most exacting model of its kind.

Time and again, I've heard clients say that their wives didn't like a certain commercial, and it was obvious that they were giving more weight to that one opinion than to anything else. Do you hear any of that?

I used to hear it a lot more. The funny thing is that people who say that sort of thing, intelligent people, never really realize what the hell they're saying. They are making uninformed, subjective judgments in areas where we have a lot of documented evidence. That's the unsophisticated marketing person, and there are very few of those left.

What about the guy who questions the effectiveness of TV commercials in general? What do you tell him?

We don't hear that question much anymore. At the moment, network television is sold out—until next spring—and that fact speaks for itself. You have to pay a higher price than you ever paid before, from $45–90,000 for a minute of network prime time, and the reason we do is that it works. It does influence people. It does move products.

Look at cigarettes. Taking them off television has really hurt them in terms of introducing new brands. It just costs so much more. If you can't use television, it's very difficult to reach people with the impact TV offers.

But there's such an absolute saturation of commercials now; it's impossible to remember what they're all saying.

None of us likes clutter. And it's true that if we went upstairs to a screening room now and looked at a bunch of commercials, you'd have a difficult time remembering what you saw after we came down. People don't "recall" commercials. But there have been enough tests to show us that they register. The mind takes pictures and stores them away.

And when your wife gets to the supermarket, she's had absolutely no way of knowing anything about that new product except what she's seeing on the shelf, and what she saw on television. No other way. We know that. Why does she reach for one item on the shelf? Does it just fall into her shopping cart? No way. When we ask her about it—and we do, at a research facility we maintain at a shopping center in Pennsylvania—she may not remember a thing about the commercial. But she buys the product. The message is getting through.

And to just the right audience, I might add. We can identify the target for a client's products and services very precisely. And then, through our media planning, we can reach any particular age group, demographic area or special interest group.

Are clients reasonably objective in judging how well you do this?

I think so. Don't forget, there's a lot of marketing and advertising savvy in American corporations. It's an absurd presumption that agencies have a monopoly on brains or creativity.

But sometimes there are arbitrary decisions. Maybe the client has a new advertising manager who says, "I'm new on the job and I'm a professional manager. I've just come from so-and-so where I worked with so-and-so and I want them. No offense to you." At first you get angry but then you think, "Well, at least we didn't waste a lot of time with him. At least he didn't make us waltz him around before he dumped us."

How do you prevent a client-agency relationship from deteriorating below professional levels? I'm thinking of the George Washington Hill type of relationship, the early days of Lucky Strike advertising.

When the client puts the agency in a complete "supplier" role—when you stop being a counselor and they don't want to listen to you—you'll run into problems. To me, the best role an agency can possibly achieve with a client is that of a trusted counselor. And if the client doesn't respect the counsel, then he'd better get another agency.

Have you resigned any accounts in recent years?
Yes, we have. Usually for fiscal reasons.

Have there been times where they simply weren't listening to you?
Yes, and if the situation deteriorates, you'll use fiscal reasons or whatever else you can as a reason to drop out. But it doesn't happen that often. Many of our clients have been with us for years; we've been AT&T's agency since it began national advertising nearly seventy years ago.

How do you develop that kind of enduring relationship with a client?
By learning his business inside out and staying on top of it, by keeping involved.

If you were a client, what could you do to encourage that sort of healthy relationship?
I'd trust them, let the agency know everything about my problems and business and welcome their initiative. That way, they're going to be much more on my side, helping me with my problems. And my problems are not just those of creating an ad. If I'm a client, I've got distribution problems, production problems, sales problems, a lot of things. But if the agency is thought of as just another vendor, all I'm going to get from them is standard fare. If I let the agency fill a larger role, on the other hand, I get a lot more. The advertising itself improves, because it comes from a larger knowledge of the business and its problems.

Besides advising a corporation executive to hire Ayer, what do you advise him about his advertising?

That his internal advertising staff is vital to him. Pay attention to hiring and developing and promoting professional people in his own advertising staffs. Don't just bring people up from the field and say, "Okay, now you're the advertising guy."

Does that still happen in big companies?

Oh, sure, sure. It's the theory of generalists. You know, that anybody can manage anything.

And your experience tells you otherwise, Lou?

Well, I've been on both sides of this business. I've been director of advertising for a division of Chrysler and I've been on the agency side. There's no doubt in my mind that if I were to go back now to Detroit, I would be able to get more productivity out of an agency because I know what they can and cannot do. And I know how to nurture an agency, how to get the best out of it.

So if I were a corporation executive, I'd hire someone out of an agency or someone who'd had agency experience. At a number of companies, the top men responsible for advertising came out of agencies or worked there at some stage of their careers. And they're very professional clients; they know what they can get out of their agencies and they know how to do it. They know how to involve us.

Lou, you're relatively new as a chief executive. How do you hope the success of your agency and yourself will be measured during your leadership?

You may find this a surprise coming from me, but I don't intend to measure the success of this agency or my own success as chief executive officer by the increase in our billings. We have been one of the fastest-growing agencies in America, but we should not use that as the mark of our success. The quality of our work is the mark of what we have done. And it will be the measure of what we do. We will grow, of course. But the goals we set for ourselves will be goals of quality, not of quantity.

We want to grow steadily—not helter skelter. As a matter of fact this has been our pattern over the past ten years.

An agency never should put itself in a position to topple from its own weight, as has happened to agencies obsessed with just increasing billings.

Nor should it try to move out of the area it knows best, as some did with bicycles and sailboats and oyster beds.

In over a hundred years, Ayer has gone through every problem of growth. The agency business as we know it today started here. Ayer literally invented it.

You've been through it all. Mistakes too?

We've made mistakes, dreadful mistakes. There was a time when this business was close to failing. If it had not been for the great effort of my predecessor, Neal O'Connor, and for the efforts of a great many of us, there might not be a NW Ayer today.

But those mistakes that hurt us so in the past are the valuable experience that now makes us a truly matured agency. An agency older than all but eight of its clients, staffed with people who are involved with their clients and with the agency itself, an agency staffed with people who think of each other and respect each other as human beings. That's the kind of agency I want to work for. That's the kind of agency I'm proud to be chairman of.

Donald V. Seibert

Chairman and Chief Executive Officer
J. C. Penney Company

With retail sales approaching $8 billion a year, J. C. Penney is one of the great success stories of American business. More than 400 full-line department stores, nearly 1,300 smaller soft-line stores, plus discount, drug, and supermarket chains, a catalog mail order business, and a life, health, and casualty insurance company make it a solid local institution throughout America.

It all began in 1902, in a small Wyoming coal mining town, when James Cash Penney invested $500 of his own money, and borrowed $1,500 from a Missouri bank, to open a store he called "The Golden Rule."

From that first store grew a nationwide corporation that's widely admired in the business community for its integrity and its able management. In 1973, *Dun's Review* named it as one of the five best-managed companies in the country.

Donald V. Seibert, Chairman of the Board and Chief Executive Officer, joined the company after World War II service. He was appointed to his present post in 1974.

J. C. Penney is known for the excellence of your planning process. What makes it unusual?

Probably its extensiveness, its thoroughness. We did our first formal five-year planning around 1963, and, since then, our projections have been updated annually. So our growth and profit plans for any particular year undergo refinement for five years before they become the basis for next year's budget. Our goal is to set guidelines for delegated decision-making, to give our operating managers an idea of what management expects, and to establish standards for budget-making at the individual stores, depending on the type of facility, the particular market, and so on.

So you do much more than set objectives for Penney as a whole.

Oh, yes. The process involves input from more than 1,600 store managers across the country. The final plan, which includes specialized guidelines for our districts and regions, takes into account the problems of each individual store. At the same time, however, our planning and research department prepares a long-range analysis that concentrates on the big picture. We study the country's 160 major metropolitan markets, analyze store locations, local demographics, and marketing trends. From that, we can determine where and what kind of new facilities to open in the next five years. And when we put that information together with the input from our stores, we can get a good idea of our capital needs and that sort of thing.

I'm wondering, though, how accurately any retailer can plan when so many factors are beyond your control. For example, what happened to your planning process when the recession hit in 1974?

Well, that sort of precipitous drop in the economy does require an immediate response. In 1974, we were in the middle of our planning process when it became clear that things were going to slide off further than we'd thought. We saw that the recession was obviously going to have an impact on us, particularly in relation to expansion planning, new space, and inventory. Inventory plans are relatively short-term; you can do something about that. But our commitments to new space presented a different kind of problem because there you're talking really about three years ahead.

In plans to open new stores, Don?

It's more than a question of planning. We generally sign a lease three years before we open a store. So we're talking about legal commitments. When the recession hit, we already had commitments until midway through 1977.

Did you decide to compensate by cutting back for 1978 and 1979? Or did you figure that the recession would be over by then and keep your plan on an even keel?
We knew that things would change, most likely for the better, by then. But the economists couldn't agree on when it would bottom out and we didn't want to commit ourselves 100 percent.

So what did you do?
First, we identified all the projects to which we were legally or morally committed. The moral commitments involved, for example, shopping center projects where we hadn't signed any papers but had given clear go-aheads to a developer; he'd already spent maybe several million dollars and we felt committed. Anyway, we distinguished between those things we didn't feel we could change and those we could defer. Some of them we simply spread over longer periods and a few we eliminated. We created what we referred to internally as our "bedrock plan."

Did you change your basic planning emphasis?
Well, yes, to the extent that we weren't sure when the economy would change and decided to focus on projects that would take less time to activate.

Such as?
We have stores in small- and middle-sized markets that require only twelve to eighteen months to get off the ground. So we have opportunities there. There's also the possibility of taking over existing space; that's a quick proposition. And our drug store division, Thrift Drug, has a very short time-line.

When the recession hit, weren't you planning a very large new catalog distribution center?
In Kansas City; that's correct. We postponed that by a year in order to balance our financial situation. But we kept the plan flexible, so we could speed up construction if things took an upturn. And we've since moved back to our original target date on that. As it turns out, the catalog part of

our business has continued to grow very rapidly. It's been growing at over 20 percent compounded over many years now, so we need that plant in Kansas City.

And you've adjusted your plans accordingly?
Yes. At the same time, though, retailing in major markets continues to be our primary source of revenue. And the recession did introduce a need for us to go back and establish a new set of priorities for those areas.

Reflecting short- or long-term uncertainty?
Reflecting the fact that, in 1977, 1978 and part of 1979, we'll be concentrating more than usual on the smaller markets. After that, we'll accelerate the full-line store program. And by then, we'll have had time to reanalyze our priorities. So I think we will have come out of the recession in good shape, maybe even with a sounder program than we had before.

Thanks, largely, to your detailed five-year planning?
Yes. Well, we call it our "five-year plan," because that's what it started out to be. But some of our projections now go a lot further. In the present "five-year plan," we're actually looking about ten years ahead, through 1987. We've made computer models, based on our current mix of business, to project where we'll be then in terms of sales, profits, and other key factors.

Looking that far ahead, though, how close to the mark can you get? Isn't it likely that your business mix will change by then?
Well, our projections, like all projections, require a good number of assumptions. In our construction budgets, for example, we may inaccurately predict inflation rates. You know, we do as well as we can, but you just can't tell exactly what will happen in the future. So in setting growth objectives for our store operations people, we tend to ignore these unknown factors.

Deliberately?
Yes. We want sales to increase by a certain percentage each year. And we see our sales goals as something to work toward. But from a financing standpoint, you must keep in mind that things happen which you can't predict or control. If you look back, you find that, on the average, you have about one bad year out of five. So we build that into our financing plan and

it works out pretty well. You know, you can't determine now that in 1982 we're going to have a bad year.

Unless you are an ostrich, you realize life isn't that predictable. You don't know exactly what will happen, when it will happen, or how severe it will be. You just decide arbitrarily that one of the next five years will be flat and you make your capital commitments with the recognition that you'll have a down year in there somewhere. It doesn't matter which one it is.

You won't be overcommitted when it comes.

Right. The problem, of course, is when you get a year like 1974, which is even worse than you'd allowed for. Then you do have to make adjustments. Still, I think the planning process we follow kept us from being in any serious trouble even then. We can go through a severe drop like that and still be in good shape.

For example, we will open more stores this year than in any single year in the history of the Penney Company going all the way back to the 1920s when we were expanding through acquisition. Our financial condition, of course, is quite good because of both our move to LIFO and our stock issue. We are quite solid. With the flexibility that we've built into the plan, even if there's a dip in 1978 and 1979, we'll take it okay as we did in 1974.

Because you can adjust quickly?

Yes, but also because we won't be overextended to begin with. We will have built enough of a conservative bias in the plan to weather that kind of drop and maintain our forward goals.

What do you find to be the most difficult aspect of planning, the greatest challenge?

Well, I think the biggest thing is to make sure that a lot of Penney people are involved in the process. After all, they're responsible for executing the plan. And if the people who are going to have to make it work are involved in its creation and are committed to it on that basis, you obviously stand a better chance of pulling it off.

In a company as large as your, how do you coordinate that involvement?

It's difficult. We have people spread all over the United States, and even within our headquarters, we sometimes have communications problems. But we have meetings where we explain our objectives to senior management and the next level. And they can then go down to their departments with a request to develop their part of the plan. They feed it back up and the whole thing comes together for review.

At what level does the involvement start? In effect, does the plan begin by saying to the store managers, through channels, that your goal for the next year is a 15 percent increase in earnings or whatever? Or does the store manager tell you what he thinks he can do and you modify it up the line?

The store manager tells us what he thinks he can do; we really don't impose what we think. Of course, he's working closely with the district manager, who understands where we want to go. So there's some coaching and dialogue there. But, essentially, we really just want to know where the stores think they're going; they're closer to the action than anybody else. We give them all kinds of information, and they understand corporate goals. But corporate goals are a composite. You can't really apply a corporate growth objective to an individual store and make any sense of it. It's even difficult to do with an entire region, because they're growing at different rates. We do, though, want to get as much information as we can from our stores—for example, what they're saying about various lines of merchandise, so we can relay that to the buying department. Then we try to put all the pieces together.

How?

Well, when all this information comes up through the organization and finally reaches the policy committee for review, we simply try to make our best judgment about what we can do. And we formulate a company plan. At which point, really, you have an obligation to go back down through the organization and explain why you modified or rejected something. If you don't communicate that successfully, your people begin to lose interest the next time around.

People figure they're not being listened to?

That's right, and you won't get as good a product. But this is the way it should be; it's completely understandable. And we know we haven't always done as good a job with this as we should. After you've made some of the tough decisions and evolved a plan, the tendency is just to print it, send it out, and relax. But to keep everybody interested and on the same team, you really have to go back and explain your rationale. That's the one area where you're most apt to make mistakes of omission, because it's additional work and doesn't always appear to have the same priority as the planning itself.

You do a lot of listening, Don, when you travel around the country visiting your stores. I'm sure you do the same with your high-level policy committees. At what point do you play an active role, a decisive role?

Sometimes we get into a situation where there is uncertainty, where it isn't clear as to which way we should go. The datum itself doesn't make the decisions for you. You have to make a judgment. When you get into that kind of situation, nobody says, "Well, what are we going to do, boss?" That doesn't really happen. What does happen is that as you discuss it with your senior people, they begin to look for some indication as to direction to go. At that point, I think it's incumbent upon the chief executive officer to express his own view.

How do you act decisively without squashing dissent?

First of all, you have to create a management climate that embraces open discussion and permits failure. You don't want anybody to feel he has stuck his neck out too far if he takes a position that you don't agree with. He's got to know that he won't lose his head if he's overruled. It's all part of the process. We try to foster open exchange and even to permit communications through unorthodox channels.

I'll give you an example. We looked at a market recently, one of the few remaining metropolitan markets where we don't have good representation of stores. We have some opportunities to get into this market during the next five years. But when we had to make a decision, the construction costs and all the other numbers added together did not project a satisfactory return on our investment. On the basis of the numbers we were looking at, we should not make the required commitments. But if we did not make these commitments, we might have precluded a reasonable entry into this market.

In that particular discussion, I found myself finally making a judgment that we needed to recognize first how much we really belong in that market. It's a good market for us. And though currently the numbers don't come out right, we needed to think we were capable of influencing the numbers over the next several years so that ultimately they will come out right. To assume we cannot improve on these things would mean in effect a decision to stay out of this market. That would be a poor management position as we look to the future. I expressed this view in our discussion, and we were able to reach a consensus in our planning.

How does the customer fit into your planning? Can you project customer trends the way you can plot changes in the economy?

To some extent, yes. For example, we've been dealing lately with the matter of how much service the customer wants and is willing to pay for. And we can get feedback on this in a variety of ways. First, by just talking to customers and finding out how they feel about it. And, too, by comparing our sales and share of the market to that of, say, a specialty dress shop. They're giving more service and charging higher prices so we watch how they are doing.

Do you find, generally, that the customer is willing to pay for more service?

It depends. If you're going to buy a high-priced camera, you want to talk to someone who understands that equipment. If you're buying a suit, you need someone who knows about alterations and all that. These areas require people. And we've found that, by adding personnel in certain departments, we can improve sales substantially. On the other hand, there are areas where customers, by their actions, have told us that they don't want to be interfered with. They just want to serve themselves. There, our obligation is simply to just make it easy for them to find what they want.

You're pinpointing exactly where the customer wants more service, where he doesn't.

Yes, and we've made this an all-out company effort. We have literally thousands of people challenging themselves about how we can combine materials and human resources to best serve the customer and improve productivity.

This brings up another point. The J. C. Penney system has always been proud of the security it gives its people. Unless they blow things pretty badly, they know they're not going to lose their jobs. In that atmosphere, how do you get people to challenge themselves? How do you give them security and yet keep them motivated?

Well, I don't think the two things are mutually exclusive. There is security in that, as long as you continue to do well at your present job here, you're not going to lose it. And if all you want is that job, it's okay. But most people aren't content just to stay at one level; and to move up, you've got to challenge yourself and stand out in the job you're doing.

You started with Penney as a shoe salesman.
Yes, and I remember that, early in my career, my goal was to manage the biggest shoe department in the company. But after I ran my first shoe department for about a year, I began to look around and see people with bigger positions and my goals started to change. I wanted to manage the whole store. Then, as I rubbed shoulders with people in higher positions, I concluded that I could aspire to those positions and I began to elevate my sights even more.

And you had to be competitive.
Well, you really need to concentrate on doing your present job as well as possible and not think continually about what the next one might be. But, yes, this is a competitive business. Just as you're competing with other retailers, you're also competing with other individuals in the Penney Company for advancement. There's a lot of aggressive application for jobs.

In-fighting?
No, it's not *that* aggressive. We very rarely see people trying to do someone else in for the sake of a job. One reason, I think is the heritage that Mr. Penney started.

He always promoted the feeling of working together. That was part of the uniqueness of his organization. He even called his people "associates" instead of employees, a custom we've continued. I think this kind of working environment effectively discourages in-fighting.

Another reason is our continuing expansion. We've always been a growth company, so there are a lot of opportunities for promotion. Particularly now. You know, fifteen years ago, becoming a store manager was the ultimate goal for most Penney people. Well, we have other opportunities today that are equally attractive. Our stores are much larger; they require professional staffs that weren't needed in the past. And now, when you talk to our people, you find that, while compensation is important, they also want responsibility. They don't want to have to run to somebody to get an okay every time they want to do something.

And that, you feel, is the heart of the whole thing?
People really have to feel that they're responsible for something, that

they can affect the success of the company. Then they discover that the best way to do that is to get the people around them to participate too. So in the end, your own people will not permit you to fail. They're going to make certain you succeed, because they have a piece of it.

In fact, you literally give your people quite a large chunk of the action. According to Dun's Review, *your compensation program is "not only innovative, but probably unique." Is incentive pay at the core of that program?*

That's right. Until 1960, no one here, including the president and chairman, drew a regular salary of more than $10,000 a year. And even now, our actual salaries are lower than most of our competitors'. The real money comes through the incentive pay, in both cash and stocks, with the amounts based on a formula that takes into account both individual and corporate performance.

Are these bonuses just for the top brass?

Not at all. The stock plan, for example, encompasses thousands of Penney people, among them our store managers. At the lower levels, of course, the amounts are relatively small. But there, it's the fact of participation, not the amount, that really matters.

Is giving people a slice of the action essentially the way you motivate people at J. C. Penney? Or is it something deeper?

Well, I think a slice of the action is important, but what it represents is more than the money itself. Because you could give people the same money in straight salary or bonuses or whatever and it wouldn't accomplish the same thing. By giving people a hand in the decision-making process and tying the money to Penney's growth, we're saying that you've earned it; you've made a contribution and it's yours.

That has been part of your company philosophy for a long time, hasn't it?

Ever since James Cash Penney opened his second store in 1903. And ten years later, when the company adopted a seven-point statement of values, one of them was to reward the men and women in our organization through participation in what the business produces. To us, that's always meant both financial compensation and the delegation of responsibility. And it's a rule we still live by.

Why isn't this the case at more companies? Isn't authoritarianism much more typical than the concept you're talking about?

Well, when people come to us from other companies, they often comment on the difference. But I really can't comment on the rightness or wrongness of somebody else's approach. I just know that, personally, I prefer to live in our kind of environment because you end up feeling good about your job. You enjoy it; it's fun to come to work in the morning. You feel important; you feel secure. I think we have enough to contend with in this life without having to come to work always wondering what's going to fall on our heads today.

Donald V. Seibert

119

Walter S. Holmes, Jr.

*Chairman of the Board
and Chief Executive Officer*
CIT Financial Corporation

To many consumers CIT Financial Corporation is not a familiar name. Nevertheless, with $7 billion in assets, 23,800 employees and more than 1,000 offices and plants, CIT ranks among America's largest companies. And many of its operating companies are indeed well known to their various publics.

Three of the firm's four divisions—Business and Consumer Financing, Insurance, and Banking—provide financial services. Through twelve principal operating companies, including National Bank of North America, these divisions account for 85–90 percent of CIT's income. A fourth division, Manufacturing and Merchandising, consists of All-Steel Inc. (office furniture), Gibson Greeting Cards, Inc., Picker Corporation (medical equipment) and Raco Inc. (electrical products). This combination of financial and manufacturing operations makes the company unique in American business.

Presiding over CIT is Walter S. Holmes, Jr., who joined the firm in 1959 as controller after having filled that same position at RCA. In 1973, three years after he became chief executive officer, Holmes was elected the fourth CIT chairman of the board since its 1908 founding.

Mr. Holmes, CIT is a giant corporation. Yet your corporate name isn't as well known as some other companies of comparable size. Why is that?

I suppose it goes back to the fact that until 1958, nearly all of our income was derived from automobile financing, industrial financing and factoring. We were best known for automobile financing, but we worked with car dealers rather than with car buyers, which limited our visibility. In industrial financing and factoring, we dealt mainly with small- and intermediate-size businesses, not with large firms or with consumers. We had no consumer products to advertise extensively.

Today, each of our operating companies maintains an identity in its own marketplace and targets its selling efforts toward a specific customer base. We think this individualized marketing strategy, rather than a corporate umbrella approach, meets our objectives best.

Few other companies have given up a billion-dollar business, as CIT did when it virtually withdrew from automobile financing, and yet have maintained earnings growth. What was the key to your successful shift out of the business?

The resources we had developed during more than sixty years in the finance industry. A highly capable field management. A nationwide network of offices. A strong capital base and enormous borrowing capacity. We were able to acquire a substantial number of consumer finance branches to supplement our program for internal growth. And we emphasized increased activity in personal loans. It took us only six years for personal loan receivables to surpass the billion-dollar mark. In addition, we were able to identify another logical area for stepped-up CIT participation—mobile homes. We built up a sizable portfolio as that industry grew.

Of course, our insurance operations and our move into banking in 1965 also were important factors in easing the transition. They gave us a diversity of earnings sources.

In addition to providing a broad range of financial services, Mr. Holmes, CIT is also involved in manufacturing. So you're really a conglomerate, aren't you?

We don't view ourselves as a conglomerate, but I suppose that could be said. If you added up the sales of our various manufacturing companies, that division would rank toward the mid-portion of the *"Fortune* 500." In terms of our total profits, on the other hand, manufacturing accounts for only ten percent. So we're primarily a multi-faceted financial institution.

Still, you do have a large manufacturing division, and I'm wondering why you launched it. Henry Ittleson, your company's founder, once said that "Products may enjoy wide use for a few years and be superseded by entirely new and better products. But credit—the commodity in which we deal—is ever in demand." In light of this statement, why move into manufacturing?

First, although credit *is* ever in demand, the specific ways in which credit can be profitably supplied do change. You can see evidence in our withdrawal from automobile financing and our introduction of several new credit products in recent years.

We made our initial entry into manufacturing in 1958 with the acquisition of Picker because we were somewhat over-capitalized at the time. For that reason, our management thought it would be advantageous to undertake some modest nonfinancial investments. We acquired Gibson Greeting Cards in 1964 and All-Steel in 1966. Raco, originally a part of All-Steel, was separated and established as a fourth manufacturing operation in 1975. Our ownership of National Bank of North America and the bank holding company legislation of 1970 precludes us from further manufacturing or merchandising acquisitions.

Has your total return on the manufacturing division been on a par with the return from your financial subsidiaries?

No, it hasn't been—yet—although the trend is moving in that direction. We're very encouraged by the developments of the past few years. But we're still not wholly satisfied with overall performance. Relative to the capital invested and to the volume generated by our manufacturing companies, there's still room for improvement. But on the whole the division has done well for us.

Your whole attitude toward acquisitions seems to typify CIT philosophy. You didn't jump in. You took your time and when you bought companies, they worked out for you. The same applies to your computer operation. You took time to introduce it, But when you did, you didn't have the problems that other firms have had. There was a thoroughness, a caution, and it's paid off. Have I characterized you correctly?

In many of our financing and banking operations, we often lead the field in terms of timing, innovative techniques and so forth. But when it comes to a major technological investment such as computers, you're right. We held off because we knew there were many problems involved in swinging over from pen and pencil to automation. And our needs were changing as a result of our move out of automobile financing. In addition, we wanted to be sure the first-generation problems were solved before we made a major commitment. While it would be an oversimplification to say that we had no problems, our move to computers was done very carefully and with a minimum of trouble.

Tell me how you did it, Mr. Holmes.

Well, unlike most companies, we didn't start out by making major investments and recruiting a lot of technicians. Todd Cole, our President, and Bob Parsons, our Vice President in charge of Systems, had both previously been with Eastern Airlines, which had the most outstanding computer set-up in its industry. Todd and Bob recognized that our requirements were similar in many respects to those of an airline reservation system.

So we worked with Eastern to wed their technology and hardware to our financing expertise. We developed a unique consumer finance computer operation that we call the "CITation System." It's a more complicated system than a company only in the personal loan business would have, because we offer a broad range of services within a complex regulatory framework that varies from state to state.

How long did it take you to develop your computer system?

A little more than two years. We set a target date for completion about eighteen months in advance and came in on time. Also, we came in within our budget. Furthermore, the success we've had with the program in terms of increasing productivity has been pretty much in line with our projections.

How, specifically, has the system helped CIT?

For one thing we've been able to keep pace with inflation because we don't have to absorb increased labor costs to the extent that we once did. Our labor needs per transaction are lower. So we can efficiently handle greater volume with the same number of people.

What's going to happen to your labor force as computer data processing takes over more and more of your paper work? Will it decline over the long term?

On the contrary, I feel that our total employment is going to increase as our volume increases. Many of the tedious, high turnover jobs will be eliminated, but the more challenging ones will increase.

In our factoring operation, for example, we're employing more people to perform qualitative services, such as credit analysis. At our bank, on the other hand, our check-sorting operation is now highly automated, so we've been able to free people from that repetitive clerical routine.

Instead of eliminating jobs, then, will computerization allow you to offer new services?
Definitely. Our revolving credit plans are an outgrowth of the computer system, for example, and we're developing a number of other new financial products based on our computer capabilities. Over the long term, there will be a number of benefits for our customers.

Such as?
As with all banks, ours is confined to a certain geographic territory, New York state. But we foresee an elimination of those boundaries and the emergence of true "national" banking in some form. Computer terminals, allowing the electronic transfer of funds, would be an important tool when that day comes.

So far, haven't the courts ruled that computer terminals are subject to the same legislation as bank branches?
Yes, but we think that will change. We also think the time will come when many of our personal loan offices will offer the types of services now available at bank branches.

Would they provide full banking services?
In terms of the scope of the services themselves, there's no reason why they couldn't. We'd have to make some modifications, but the essential technology for this is already in place.

How far in the future might this happen?
It's difficult to establish a timetable because things are changing much faster than generally anticipated. Traditions are breaking down very quickly. That's not only because of technology, but because our population has become more mobile. People travel much more, and they're less insular in their thinking.

If you had real nationwide competition in the banking industry, how would the consumer be affected? Would loan rates be likely to go down, for example?

I think the public would significantly benefit. In fact, increased banking competition has already begun to profit the consumer. Here in New York, for example, the legislature has permitted savings and loan institutions to offer checking accounts, provided they don't charge for the service. As a result, our commercial bank has begun to offer no-charge checking accounts, too.

Do you feel that other lines of demarcation between commercial banks and savings and loan institutions should be broken down?

Yes, I was a member of the Presidential Commission on Financial Structure and Regulation, which made a two-year study (1970–72) of nancial institutions. And that was one of our recommendations.

Because CIT covers nearly every aspect of financial needs, the full implementation of that recommendation wouldn't really hurt you, would it? Even if your competitive position declined, you could compensate with your personal loan business.

Not really, because savings and loan institutions, which had been primarily mortgage-oriented, are now getting the capability to make personal loans. So new competition is opening up in that area. Nevertheless, for the total good of the consumer and the country, I feel that lines of demarcation should be eliminated. And that was the consensus of the commission, provided all financial institutions are permitted to operate under the same ground rules, namely, equality of taxation, regulation and supervision.

From your comments, I gather that the commission took a very broad view of the public interest.

There was some advocacy of positions, but for the most part the commission's members tried to cast aside their parochial points of view. It was a diverse, balanced group, with members representing the public as well as specific industries. Even if someone had wanted to favor a certain industry, I don't think he could've gotten away with it.

What about your legislative interests? Have you or other CIT officials had occasion to testify before Congressional committees on matters of monetary policy or whatever?

We did testify in regard to bank holding company legislation, but for the most part, we've felt that our positions are best presented by industry groups. The American Bankers Association, for example, is an effective group. And in consumer lending, the National Consumer Finance Association and the various state associations do a good job of communicating to the state regulators. We prefer to work through organizations like those.

When you talk to the people who do present your case, what do they say about the legislators and regulators? Do the government people seem to listen sympathetically to the industry's problems? I'm not asking whether they always agree with you, but whether they appear responsible in their attitudes.

It depends on the individual. Some are very responsive. I don't mean that they necessarily accede to what the industry wants, but they respect our viewpoints.

In consumer finance, the state regulatory agencies, perhaps because they're close to the field, seem to have a good understanding of competitive conditions. In addition, we find a high degree of objectivity in the Federal Reserve Board.

Let's move on to another subject. How can you do long-range planning when the key factors in the money markets are dependent on political and economic factors which are utterly beyond your control?

We obviously have the same kinds of problems in analyzing the future as everybody else. We can only do our best. And particularly with long-range plans, we expect actual results to show variation.

How far ahead do your financial plans go?

Five years, though some of our companies are on three-year plans.

What philosophy underlies your financial planning, Mr. Holmes?

We try to keep a balance between long- and short-term borrowing, because we need both the stability afforded by the long-term and the flexibility that goes with the short-term. Borrowing, of course, is related to our equity base, which is now more than $800 million. Our borrowings presently total just under $3 billion, about 45 percent of which is short-term. So there's a 3.0 to 1 ratio between total borrowing and the equity base.

The important thing is to keep nimble. In putting our money to work, we want to avoid the obvious trap of borrowing short-term and lending long-term. We try to balance the borrowing and lending to give ourselves protection against factors that can't be determined.

Does your crystal ball show the imminent capital shortage that everyone is talking about?

I think the shortage is exaggerated, particularly in today's money market where everybody's looking for places to put their money to work.

I do think that over the longer term, money is going to become a more difficult commodity to obtain. But I also believe that companies with a strong financial structure will still be able to attract funds. It's the marginal operations that will feel the pinch, not the companies of our stature. Still, I think there's no doubt that companies will be paying more and more for money.

Is that belief leading you to do more long-term borrowing?

Certainly we like to protect ourselves as much as possible. And over the past few years, we have increased the percentage of our borrowing that is long-term. But the possibility of an intensified capital shortage isn't the only reason for that. Our asset mix, for one thing, has become more weighted toward industrial financing. As a result, we're making more long-term investments. And that means an increase in long-term borrowing.

Another factor has been the withdrawal from automobile financing, and our increased involvement in the personal loan business. Our auto financing was relatively short-term in that we could turn over funds in two or three years. By contrast, while our obligations on any one personal loan are also short-term, there's a high tendency for our customers to stay with us and borrow again. So we, in turn, tend to fund that business with money that we've borrowed long-term.

In effect, you're giving customers lines of credit similar to what a business would have. Is that correct?

That's basically what's happening today as we establish so-called "revolving credit" plans in more and more states.

It's a pretty new trend, isn't it, Mr. Holmes?

In the personal loan business, yes. In part, I think, it's a reaction to the rise of the credit card. It's also a way to minimize the cost involved in servicing accounts. With today's mobile population and our nationwide system of branches all tied together in one computer system, revolving credit makes perfect sense. If we serve a customer in New Jersey and he moves to Utah or wherever, we can still serve him.

What kind of people would get in the habit of borrowing and have a need for revolving credit? Is it just the nature of things that some people can't manage their money?

No, it's just the nature of the way the world works today. It's a credit world, and there's nothing sinful about borrowing money. The automobile industry was built on the basis of credit.

Has your experience with borrowers been generally good?

Very good. The American public is honest. Our consumer credit losses have been under two percent of total receivables outstanding. Of course, our criteria for granting credit are prudent. We lend only to people who have the capability to repay. Even the person who has assumed a number of debts may well have a good job and own a home in which he has equity. When the lender is prudent, financing is a very sound business.

Credit lines aside, what did your manufacturers have to gain from your ownership? They're involved in wholly different industries from those that primarily concern CIT.

First of all, CIT's corporate management doesn't pretend to have operating expertise in X-ray products, office furniture, greeting cards, electrical products or any of our other manufacturing lines. We look on our role as one of stimulating the managements of our specialized companies. We have been able to accelerate their growth. There were no unfriendly takeovers by CIT and the companies were all sound. Their managements saw an opportunity to grow much faster under us than would have been possible if they'd remained independent.

Of course, our successes wouldn't have been possible if we hadn't begun with a very careful selection process. We started by making sure that each company is managed by the best available people.

Numbers aside, how do you evaluate your companies?

Numbers *are* important, but a lot of intangibles come into play, too. The character of people, leadership capabilities, mutual confidence and so on.

A company like Gibson, for example, wouldn't tend to employ the same kinds of people that you'd expect to find at a financial corporation. So evaluation is complex. It takes time. But we only acquired companies that had already demonstrated expertise in their management through performance. That made our job a lot easier.

Also, to reiterate, we only acquired companies that wanted to join CIT, with people who wanted to work with us. So there was a compatibility to begin with.

How do you nurture it?

We combine close centralized monitoring with a decentralized operating approach. Several of us from CIT are members of each company's board alongside its own management. The directors meet monthly to review operating results, management forecasts, forward planning and general policy matters. Each company's president and chief executive officer directs day-to-day activities. They're assisted by a management staff that includes specialists with broad expertise in the company's industry. They develop comprehensive operational objectives and financial budgets. And after review and approval they're responsible for execution of the plans.

You said that CIT executives sit on each manufacturer's board. Does it ever work the other way around?

Yes. Harvey Picker, for example, joined CIT's board when the Picker Corporation was acquired by CIT, and he's still on it. He's also dean of Columbia University's Faculty of International Affairs, and he continues as chairman of Picker Corporation. In addition, he recently was elected to the board of National Bank of North America. His broad international experience provides added counsel to the bank's international lending activities.

From your tone of voice, I suspect that you really get along with him.

That's certainly true. But I can also frankly say that initially there were some adjustment problems with the Picker Corporation. Its managers had been reared in a family-company atmosphere. And as the firm got larger a more formal structure became necessary. There was a transition period to go through.

What sort of informalities did you have to phase out at Picker?

The company was structured as a series of separate subsidiaries. In many territories where Picker operated, local management had a 15 or 20 percent stake in the area's operation. They had extensive autonomy. So as a publicly-owned company, we found ourselves dealing with a wide array of management philosophies not totally conducive to the development of a strong national marketing organization.

Bit by bit, therefore, we had to persuade local managements that it would be in our mutual best interests for them to exchange their minority ownerships for other types of compensation arrangements. Some people couldn't be persuaded, and there were cases where we had to wait for employees to retire. But most of them went along with us. Today, Picker has a much simplified and more efficient corporate structure.

The original set-up gave Picker's local management a stake in the action. How did you convince so many of them to give that up?

We were able to demonstrate that their opportunities under the new management philosophy would be much broader. And I don't think there's any doubt that they're better off now.

We introduced a more modern compensation system, for example, and increased opportunities for advancement. Many of Picker's key people have come up through its field organization since the acquisition. Under the old system, a person might have become top man in a given territory but probably wouldn't have been able to go beyond that.

Today, would someone at Picker be able to move up not only within that organization but also to a position in one of your other companies?

Absolutely. We're able to move people as quickly as they can absorb the challenges. And particularly in the past five years, we've been able to advance management development through inter-company transfers.

One executive who joined Picker several years ago as a labor relations expert now fills that role with All-Steel and Raco. In another case, we took an executive who'd been CIT's internal audit manager and made him corporate controller at Picker. Then, after several very successful years with them, he rejoined CIT as corporate controller here.

In the final analysis, the progress of the company depends on our ability to identify qualified people and develop them to their full potential. That has been said many times, of course, but business success really does rest on individual effort.

Howard B. Johnson

*Chairman of the Board and President
and Chief Executive Officer*
Howard Johnson Company

Taking over operation of a small store with 500 borrowed dollars in 1925, Howard D. Johnson launched the now-famous restaurant chain which still bears his name. He manufactured his own ice cream in a wide variety of flavors, implemented high quality-control standards and, as the business proliferated, made franchising arrangements that further hastened its growth.

Howard B. Johnson, the son of the founder, became fascinated with the burgeoning operation while he was still a young child. In 1939, at the age of only seven, he began accompanying his father on business trips. By age 12, the younger Johnson was sitting in on company meetings. And during his teen years, he spent summer vacations scooping ice cream and cutting meat in his father's restaurants and commissaries.

Having earned a BA degree from Yale and attended the Harvard Graduate School of Business Administration by 1957, Howard B. Johnson joined the company as a vice president after two years in the United States Navy. Two years later, at the age of just twenty-six, he became president and chief operating officer. In 1968, four years before his father's death, he was elected chairman of the board.

In the time that the younger Johnson has headed the firm, its annual sales and revenues have jumped from $75 million to more than $450 million. The company, and its licensees now employ 40,000 employees. It presently owns or licenses about 1,400 Howard Johnson's Restaurants and Motor Lodges, plus over 100 Ground Round and Red Coach Grill Restaurants.

Do you eat in Howard Johnson's Restaurants?

Well, I don't travel as much as I used to, but I often visit some of our franchise units. And I try products. When I go up to our headquarters in Boston, I usually eat all my meals in Red Coaches, Ground Rounds or Howard Johnson's.

Do you also stay at your own Motor Lodges, Mr. Johnson?

I do in some cases. Other times, I stay at hotels that I think are doing a particularly good job. I want to see how the competition is doing, and I always like to see their prices, because they're usually three or four times higher than ours. That makes me feel good.

When you're testing out your facilities, do you ever talk to, say, a woman behind a restaurant counter or a maid in a lodge?

When I get a chance, but it's difficult because I just don't have the time to be around much. A lot of them don't even realize there is a Howard Johnson. They think it's just a brand name.

Is that a common misconception?

Very. I remember one instance in particular.

Tell me about it, Mr. Johnson.

Well, I sometimes make surprise inspections at my restaurants. I just walk right in, pull things out of the freezer and so on. I was doing that one night at one of our restaurants in Boston, and the manager came up to me with a policeman. The manager asked me what I thought I was doing in there. I said, "I'm Howard Johnson." He said, "And I'm Christopher Columbus." And he asked the policeman to remove me from the building. I didn't have any identification, so I had to call the office and be identified.

When you're not mistaken for an intruder and do manage to talk to the people at the bottom level, what impressions do you get from them?

That they're working awfully hard. And that we're in a very tough business in terms of physical and time demands. It's a peak-and-valley type of business where, during the peak periods, everybody's working in hot kitchens or surrounded by customers who want everything in an instant.

I also recognize that a lot of our employees might not be crazy about their jobs. They're doing it for a living. But we still have to try to project an atmosphere where you can walk in and immediately feel that every employee is a believer. I think the airlines and Walt Disney do that dramatically. McDonald's does it to some degree. But not many companies do it well. And when you've got over 1,400 company-owned and franchised units, it's very difficult.

I've heard it said that, in general, franchised operations are better managed and more profitable than company-owned units. Is this true at Howard Johnson's?

We have some extraordinarily well-run franchise units. But while they may have higher sales volumes than some of the company ones, the company units tend to make more money.

You haven't found, then, that the entrepreneur who has his own money at stake works harder than the company-employed manager?

Well, that might be true. But the company unit still makes more money, because of tighter controls and policies.

According to what I've read, your present policy is to emphasize the short-term. You've said that, if you soundly handle that, the long-term will take care of itself. What's the thinking behind that philosophy, Mr. Johnson?

A decade or two ago, one could look into the future and predict relatively well. Management could lay out figures and then, depending on known facts, expand them over three, five or ten years. I think it's quite obvious that that's no longer possible. Predicting earnings beyond about twenty-four months is becoming more and more difficult.

As a result, all of us in American business have had to rewrite our long-range plans and concentrate more on the present and immediate future. We've had to take a whole new approach to planning, not only in terms of predicting sales and earnings, but with regard to estimating return on investment and the availability of the parts needed to make the whole.

In other words, long-term planning would be great, but the uncertainty of the outside world has made it impractical for you.

Yes, and I think we can identify inflation as what most caused us to change our concepts. For forty years, the inflation rate was around 2 percent and then, suddenly, it was 6, 9 and 12 percent. Also, I think we had a real shock when Americans discovered our dependency on other people for certain raw materials. Energy, particularly, in my business.

Especially in this current ten-year stretch, therefore, I think it's most important to take care of immediate needs, to try to run a sound business this year and next. Because we're just not able to make very good long-range projections right now.

What's the practical effect of your emphasis on the short term? What specific areas do you minimize?

We're almost a $500 million company now, and a firm of that size would generally be asking itself how to diversify and get to a billion dollars. But I've put diversification on a back-burner.

In these difficult times, my feeling is that we'd better run what we know, rather than experiment with buying businesses that may be dissimilar to ours. The risks in that are so much greater today than they were ten years ago. And if you read about conglomerates, you see how difficult it is to get a group of people to learn more than one business well.

Well, bigness has caused difficulties even for firms that engage in only one business. Some of your food franchise competitors, for example, have had trouble maintaining quality controls. Why haven't you had that problem, Mr. Johnson?

It's certainly a problem that comes with bigness. And one of the many intelligent thoughts that my dad passed along to me was that size isn't necessarily what we're trying to accomplish. We're trying to maintain a certain level of standard performance in as many units as we can. To overextend ourselves would be pointless.

You know, opening a new restaurant is always exciting—we've given birth to a new entity—but what's important is running that place for the next fifty years, which is usually the term of the lease. We've given a lot of thought to that. And consequently, while we like to grow with the rest of them, we may grow more slowly and with more certainty than some of our competitors.

Was your father a major influence in this respect?

No question about it. For many years, he preached to me that he thought it had a great deal to do with the egos of men that they emphasized growth over conservative financing. And he prevailed upon me not to suddenly decide that I had all the answers in the food business and could just build and build forever.

So when he was good enough to give me the command, I knew enough to approach expansion from a conservative position. I felt we had a lot of growth in front of us, but I didn't want to borrow heavily to do it. I wanted to do it out of cash flow.

How easy was it for you to stick with that decision?

I had a difficult time because, being a young man, I wanted to grab our growth opportunities and expand very rapidly. But I maintained an inner control, and we grew only within the limits of our cash flow.

Many of our competitors, of course, have taken a different direction and leveraged their companies a great deal. McDonald's, for example, is now almost a billion dollars in debt between leases and mortgages. They've done fabulously well with that approach, but many other companies have fallen by the wayside. And overall, I've felt that my set of values offers the soundest method of operation.

The record indicates that you've really concentrated on the bottom line—net earnings—rather than on volume.

That's correct. With inflation, the costs of money, people, food and fuel can all rise very quickly. So I believe in financial conservatism and stability and in having a high degree of liquidity on the balance sheet.

With $78 million in marketable securities, you certainly have liquidity. Why are you sitting on all that money?

We're preparing ourselves for a rather major shift in the asset/liability relationship on our balance sheet.

Let me explain. Most of the approximately 650 company-owned Howard Johnson's restaurants are on property that we lease from a landlord. At present, those leases don't appear on our balance sheet and we show a 3.5 to 1 current ratio.

We anticipate, however, that by 1980, all leases—which constitute a $250 million debt for us—will be capitalized on the balance sheet. That would drop our ratio to two to one which is very decent, but not outstanding like today's figure. Because we want to still have a very strong liquidity factor after those leases are capitalized, we'd like to have $125 million in marketable securities by 1980.

To balance the $250 million debt on the balance sheet?

That's correct. Under the new Accounting Board standards we anticipate the first year of a lease would be figured as current liability but the rest would go on the balance sheet as long-term debt. And there's always the next year's rent coming up, so we'll need twice as many assets overall to end up with a two to one current ratio. I'd like to maintain an even better ratio, but I recognize that it's going to be increasingly difficult for us to keep the figure where I'd like it.

Why is high liquidity so important to you?

Because of the ease with which it permits us to deal with expensive problems and act on expensive opportunities. It enables us to act without borrowing, with interest-free money. When I get the chance to buy something at 50 cents on the dollar, I have the cash to jump in and do it, thereby balancing against the doubling effect of inflation.

This year, for example, we were able to utilize our cash to take advantage of ten very fabulous deals where our return on investment promises to far exceed our usual performance. We're also in a position to buy out franchises from people who might want to retire. In addition, we'll always want to build thirty to fifty new restaurants every year, and they're costing maybe twice as much as they did ten years ago.

What's today's price tag for building and opening a new Howard Johnson's Restaurant?

Well, if we pay for everything, it approaches $600,000. But usually the landlord will buy the land and put up the building, so our cost might be $175,000 for equipment. We get more bang for our bucks that way.

Even so, if we have to borrow our $175,000 at ten or 11 percent interest, we're going to have to do extraordinarily well on the restaurant to make the return on investment look decent. So I think our extra cash potential is very important. I'd rather take a conservative approach than finance through extensive borrowing.

Other than in the financial area, would you say you run a conservative operation?

Oh, I think so. Our ice cream standards, for example, have been maintained through our fifty years at a very high quality. And our Motor Lodge rooms are a little better quality than those of our competition.

You're using the word "conservative" to mean high quality?

Yes, because conservative management to me partly means, don't risk the product. We've always gone for the best, most noticeable locations and tried to maintain high standards for the products. I feel strongly that, if you can do that and still have a price/value relationship that the public recognizes, you can stay in business a long time.

What about people? How does a conservative management philosophy apply to selecting, training and handling employees?

Well, whereas I'm rather formal in my habits and lifestyle, I'm informal in terms of organizational structure. Instead of having two or three men report to me, I might work with thirty or forty. Because I like to have a personal relationship with as many people as I can.

Obviously, as we get bigger, that gets more difficult. But I think everyone knows my presence and understands that I'm intently involved with a lot of material that most chief executives don't look at. I think its important that people here see how I feel and think about the company.

Do you make most of the decisions?

Most of the major ones, yes. I make a lot of them from experience, from gut feeling and from a very good knowledge of what's going on day-to-day.

Why don't you delegate more decision-making?

Because I feel that a company should be flexible enough to react to problems quickly. And in this company, we can get instant decision-making simply by picking up a phone and calling me. We don't have to go through all kinds of committees.

Of course, we do have a very capable group of people who refine my raw decisions. They do a great job and all participate at a high level. I do a lot of thinking out loud with them about where we're headed. Not that I'm trying to overwhelm them with my point of view. It isn't totally authoritative. I just want to talk things out and, if they find anything fuzzy, I want them to come back and help me reshape it.

When they do, are they rewarded?

Yes. I'm a great believer in surprise bonuses and in telling people when they've done a good job—or a bad one. I like to be candid so they know where they stand.

How candidly do your key people talk to you? Are they frightened away by your impressive title and performance or by the fact that you tend to be formal in your personality?

I think that's happened to some extent. I'd be naive to believe otherwise. I've been told on more than one occasion that I have a very strong, dominating personality when it comes to this business. So I think there's some caution taken when people approach me.

How do you deal with that?

I try to keep discussions lively and amusing to take away the tension and the stiffness. And even though I have a tendency to be a little formal, I think the fellows know that, on a one-to-one basis, we can work out a problem to the satisfaction of both of us.

Did you adopt your formal style in order to establish your authority after becoming president at a young age? Or has it always been a natural part of your personality?

The latter. In fact, I think I've gotten more formal over the years. It's just the way Howard B. Johnson assumes a leadership role.

Can you think of a time where one of your people opened up to you in a way that gave you new insights on the company?

Well, a couple of our senior vice presidents came to me two years ago and said, "We want to discuss a subject that we realize is very near and dear to your heart. We feel that we're over-controlling our restaurant business to the point where marketing and sales growth are being stifled." They recommended that we open up a little and give people more freedom of decision in the field. They knew I hadn't thought this way and that taking a chance on trying to turn me around might be harmful to their careers.

Was it?

No. We did just exactly as they suggested and, partly as a result, the company has shot forward. They were rewarded financially, by the way. And I freely give them credit for many of the things that have happened since.

Was that situation unusual? Or have a lot of this company's ideas come from people other than you and your father?

Fortunately, in a somewhat mysterious and unplanned way, we've managed to have about twenty-five important people here over the fifty-year cycle. People who have brought something to the company that propelled us another step. One brought the idea of frozen foods. Another brought the motor lodge concept. Another helped us improve our financial controls. And so on. And we had three outstanding lawyers. All of them happened to be Irish-Americans.

Then you've generally had good management people?
Yes, but not so much through an evolutionary process of hiring college graduates and developing them. It's been more haphazard than that. We were just lucky enough to have people come along at the right times. A lot of them, I think, were attracted to my father, who was a very unusual human being to work for and with.

In what respect?
He was able to bring out the best in people relative to how they operated within the company. And people listened to him, because he had an extraordinary ability to say intelligent things, to come up with creative ideas in areas like law and engineering. He could take a lease, for example, and develop it with an incredible feeling for the practical side of leasing. And yet he'd had no education at all.

I don't have that creative ability. I think my ability is that I recognize that what my father did was awfully good. And I don't need to change it for change's sake—which would be a tremendous waste of time, energy and money. Rather, I think I learned the business well enough so that I can reshape it to fit the times. I think that's what a second player on a team is supposed to do.

How old were you when you began thinking in terms of following in your father's footsteps?
It was clear to me by about the age of ten.

You've got to realize that my father and I had a rather unique relationship. When the business was in its formative years, we lived under pretty tight restrictions. And he used to tell me, when I was very young, of all the difficulties he had with the company. We used to talk about this day in and day out, before and after dinner and into the night. So I had a chance to discuss all the elements of the business with him.

It must have made a tremendous impression on me during childhood that, once you have something started, the second and third generations ought to spend a lot of time taking care of it. And my father gave me a chance to do that, which most people of his type would never do.

Your father remained chairman until 1968?

Yes, but I actually served as chairman from about 1961 on. I ran all the annual meetings, for example.

And finally one day, I called him up and said, "Dad, I think I should be chairman." He said okay, and that was the end of the conversation. It was as simple as that.

You said that you've been running the annual meetings since 1961. What problems have you encountered in communicating with the stockholders?

Nothing worth mentioning. I wouldn't call it a love affair, but we've had a very satisfactory relationship at these meetings. I generally give a short talk and then take questions. And people usually come up afterwards to say they like the way I run the meetings.

What do you tell them about your low dividend pay-outs? Has your return on stockholders' equity justified your keeping most of it? In other words, have you done better with it than they would likely have done themselves?

Well, we can either invest that money and try to do better than they would or we can increase the dividend. We're trying to do a little of both. As we mentioned in the last annual report, we've increased the dividend pay-out five times since 1967. And we're looking at the possibility of increasing it again.

One thing your annual reports don't mention is social responsibility. Yet, as you've indicated, you're particularly susceptible in your business to environmental and social factors of the outside world.

I do think external forces are becoming more and more meaningful, but how much of this should go in the annual report is questionable. I think I probably mentioned in last year's report that earnings were down because of outside forces. But I don't dwell on social responsibility, because I'm a fundamentalist in that I think annual reports—and American business—should dwell on sales and earnings.

What is Howard Johnson's proper role in regard to social responsibility?

As you know, this subject is filled with all kinds of pitfalls. It's the kind of thing where, no matter what you say, you can look bad.

Some economists believe that the biggest social contribution a company can make is to turn a profit.

Well, that's about where I stand. My job is to make a profit. I give my taxes to Uncle Sam and he spends it to improve social conditions. Also, I'm employing 25,000 people directly; more through our licensees. So I'm contributing to the growth of the gross national product.

How much more can I do? I honestly feel that I don't have the time in a competitive society to go much beyond that. I guess you could say, from a sociological viewpoint, that if I hired 50 percent Negro and 50 percent white, I might be contributing more. We don't hire on that basis, but we believe in equal opportunity and I think we've made some strides in that direction.

Do you have an affirmative action plan?
No.

How much success have you had, then, in moving women and minorities up through the ranks?

I think we're doing a better job with women than with minorities. Some of our best managers and staff heads are women and, while we haven't given much line control to women yet, I think that's coming. We already have women in some very sensitive areas.

Such as?

Well, menu planning and banquet planning. And our cash manager is a woman.

I think all restaurant companies are moving women up, particularly in the store management field and then beyond that. You know, gals have some attributes that men don't have. They like to keep cleaner kitchens, generally speaking. They're a little fussier in terms of orderliness and cleanliness. And they have more of a flair for appearances. So I think there will be some very fine positions for the gals now coming along.

Do you have any women corporate officers?

No, there's only an assistant secretary at the moment. But I think we're now putting some gals into a position where they could become corporate officers.

What about minorities? Are they moving up through management?
We have some Spanish-speaking people and a rather broad range of Negroes, including two or three who are area managers, which is our line position out in the field.

Two or three out of how many?
Oh, about seventy. We have no Negro corporate officers.

Will you have some in the future?
Possibly. It will probably take longer than with the women. You know, it has a lot to do with ability. We've given chances to some of these people, but I haven't really felt that one is ready for a general manager's role in the field. Maybe it's because we haven't got enough coming along.

Would I be wrong in sensing that this hasn't been a high priority for you?
No, you'd be right.

Okay, what problems do have a high priority with you at the moment? What ones give you the most anxiety and keep you awake at night?
I have two. One is the energy problem the United States faces over the next twenty years and how it relates to my business. The second question I'm grappling with is, "Can a man of my management style develop a second man to take his place?" I'm having a very hard time with that.

Why?
I have a very competent group of senior executives, but many of them are specialists. There are good financial men and also the creative types who don't really care that much about numbers. But it's awfully hard to get both. And I've yet to find the theoretical ideal man who has everything—including twice as much energy as I've got and the ability to run this company better than I can. If I could identify him, I'd have a tremendous sense of long-term strength.

Are you sure such a man exists?
Well, I spend a good deal of time wondering about it. But I have to believe that he's out there to be bought or that we can grow him within the company. Otherwise, there wouldn't be much point to my job.
If I get hit by a car tomorrow, of course, the Howard Johnson Company

isn't going to just stop dead in its tracks. Somebody will run it and they'll do either better or worse than I've done. It's as simple as that. Still, because I'm dedicated to the improvement of the company, I'm looking for someone who may be difficult to find.

Suppose you found him, Mr. Johnson. Might he be a psychological threat to you?

That's a distinct possibility, although I have so much going for me that I shouldn't be insecure about him. Even so, I have so many aces that the fellow who plays the game with me starts out in a pretty bad position. And I'm not sure that my management style will let him develop within the company. Because I may tend to mother it too much.

If you found this ideal man in five or ten years, would you think about stepping down? You're still young, but you've already been running this company for almost 20 years.

That's true. But I've discovered that I need this business to enjoy my life. I find it very fascinating, very stimulating. Sometimes I find it tiring and I get fed up. But when everything's considered, I must like it a great deal because I need it and I enjoy it.

On behalf of the stockholders, I have to ask myself whether I can sustain the kind of management thrust over the next 20 years needed to again double or triple the company's size. If I think that I can, I'll stay.

Forty years as chief executive?

Right, if I continue to feel healthy and excited. After twenty years, forty doesn't seem too long.

Dr. Armand Hammer

*Chairman of the Board
and Chief Executive Officer*
Occidental Petroleum Corporation

Into his seventy-plus years, Dr. Armand Hammer has successfully packed a dazzling array of activities. He has enjoyed close relationships with numerous US Presidents and foreign leaders, influenced the economies of many nations and scored triumphs with all of the diverse enterprises he has tackled.

Born of immigrant parents in New York's Lower East Side, Dr. Hammer became a self-made millionaire while still an undergraduate at Columbia University. Then, when he was barely out of his teens, he went to Russia, developed friendships with Lenin and Trotsky, and won concessions to represent thirty-eight US firms in the USSR. Returning to America

shortly after the Depression hit, he made additional millions as an art dealer, whiskey manufacturer and cattle breeder.

When he decided to retire, in 1956, his tax counsel advised him to invest in a money-losing tax shelter. Dr. Hammer chose the seemingly hopeless Occidental Petroleum Corporation which then employed just three people and had a total net worth of $34,000. Less than two decades later, Occidental recorded annual net sales of over $5 billion and rated as the 20th largest corporation in America.

Worldwide exploration for and development, production and transportation of oil, gas, coal and other natural resources constitute the firm's major activities. But Occidental, as owner of Hooker Chemical Corporation, also manufactures and distributes industrial chemicals and plastics, metal-finishing chemicals and equipment, and agricultural chemicals and fertilizers.

Dr. Hammer, who some years ago arranged an unprecedented $20 billion trade deal with the Soviets, may be described by some people as a very lucky man. As he has noted, however, "Good opportunities should never be confused with good luck. In the business world, luck goes mostly to those who work the hardest, travel the farthest and apply themselves with the most dedication."

When you first went to Russia, Dr. Hammer, you were just twenty-three and that country was an almost unknown quantity to the western world. What motivated you to go there?

Well, I'd just graduated from Columbia Medical School and I had six months to fill before beginning an internship at Bellevue Hospital. I'd sold the pharmaceutical business I'd been operating. So I had time and a good deal of money. And I wanted to do something useful.

What did you have in mind?

Russia was suffering from famine and from cholera and typhoid epidemics. So I bought a World War One surplus field hospital, a quantity of medical supplies and an ambulance, and I headed off to Moscow to see if I could be of any help.

What did you find there?

A very dismal city. Poverty, a lot of disease, very little food. I tried to see some officials, but nobody was available right away. And the Russians put me in a hotel called the Savoy, where I roomed with rats, mice and bedbugs. It was a very discouraging start.

But I hung on. I discovered what turned out to be a food speakeasy, so I started eating better. I was determined to learn 100 words of Russian per day. And finally, I managed an interview with the Commissar of Public Health, who let me join a group of observers on a fact-finding trip to the Urals.

Can you recall your impressions of that trip?

Oh, yes, quite vividly. What I saw was extraordinary in two respects.

On the one hand, the famine there was much worse than what I'd seen in Moscow. People by the hundreds were begging for food. We saw huge common graves, and even heard rumors of cannibalism. In the midst of this tragedy, though, I saw stocks of platinum, emeralds, valuable furs, all sorts of exportable commodities. I couldn't believe it.

Why hadn't the Russians traded these items abroad for grain?

That's what I kept asking them. They told me that the European blockade against Russia had only just been lifted and that it would take too long to make the trade.

Meanwhile, I knew, there'd been a gigantic grain crop in the US, and the price there was down to a dollar a bushel. Farmers in America, not wanting to go to market at that price, were actually burning their crops. And these people were starving!

What did you do?

Well, they told me it would take a million bushels of wheat to save the area I was in until the next harvest. I had a million dollars, so I made a contract to ship them the wheat, and they agreed to send me a return cargo of furs and other goods, and pay me a modest commission. I cabled my brother to buy the wheat and ship it immediately, which he did.

A few days later, a telegram arrived from Lenin. He wanted to know whether he'd heard correctly about the young American who'd reportedly arranged grain shipments for the Urals.

That's right. And when I got back to Moscow, he called me in to see him. He talked to me in fluent English and he told me that the US and Russia were complementary. He said Russia needed the technology and equipment that we could provide. And that the US could find a wide-open market in his country.

Judging from what I've read, Lenin never expected any ideological agreement with you. He simply accepted you as an American capitalist, the first to deal with Russia.

That was the way he approached me. And when I mentioned an asbestos proposition that someone had talked about on the trip to the Urals, he said that someone must break the ice. He suggested I take the first foreign concession.

Did you?

Well, I hesitated, because of what I'd seen of the Russan bureaucracy. I thought I'd be wading through red tape for months. But Lenin assured me that that wouldn't happen. He appointed a special committee, and he promised me his full cooperation.

Apparently, you got it. Lenin's letters and memos contain repeated directives to his staff and associates to treat you well. Let me quote a few of them. At one point, he told his Minister of Foreign Trade, "It is absolutely necessary that you pay strict attention to the factual carrying out of our obligations to Dr. Hammer." To Stalin, he wrote, "I ask all members of the Central Committee to fully support Dr. Hammer's enterprise."

He really was as good as his word. When I prepared the concession agreement, the Russians signed it with few changes. They also put me in a palatial guest house with excellent cuisine. And they offered me a four-story building in the center of Moscow for my headquarters.

US diplomatic recognition of the Soviet Union was still a dozen years away in 1921. But later that year, only months after signing the asbestos deal, you worked out another extraordinary arrangement. You brought the Soviets together with fervent anti-communist Henry Ford. How did you manage that?

I contacted my uncle, who'd owned a Ford agency in pre-revolutionary Russia. He arranged for me to meet with Henry Ford, and I went to Detroit. I told Ford how the Russian market could be very big for his company. But, at first, he wouldn't hear of it. He said that he would do no business there until the communist government was replaced.

What did you say to that?

That if that was the case, he had a long wait in store. I told him that the Russian people seemed to be behind Lenin and that the government there was quite stable. I also told him that, ideological questions aside, he himself was very much respected by the Russians.

Finally, he agreed to sell his products there, with me as his sole agent. After that, it was relatively easy for me to work out similar arrangements with US Rubber, American Tool Works, Ingersoll-Rand and other US companies.

By the time Lenin died, how many such contracts did you have?

Well, I was serving as sole agent for thirty-eight companies. But Stalin was much less accessible than Lenin had been. The bureaucracy was getting worse. By 1924, also, the government had become so much more interested in building up internal production that they deemed it desirable to cut down their purchases abroad. Besides, they had formed their own trading company in the US, the Amtorg Trading Company.

Did they cancel your contracts?

They first offered me a participation in Amtorg, which I declined. Then they offered me any manufacturing concession I wanted in exchange for my trading concern.

And I considered leaving Russia. But as I was thinking about this, I happened to stop by a stationery store for a pencil. And that gave me an idea.

I knew the Russians were trying to teach people to read and write, but they had no pencil factories. The same pencils that sold in the US for a nickel were selling in Moscow for 50 cents to a dollar. So I offered to set up a pencil factory.

Had you had any experience in pencil manufacture?

No, but I knew where to find it. And by attracting experts from Germany, I was able to manufacture all the pencils they needed. In fact, we had enough so that we could even export.

After you returned to the United States, you continued to prosper—to put it mildly—in a dazzling variety of fields. You made fortunes in the art world, in the whiskey business and as a cattle farmer. Why do you think you succeeded so repeatedly?

The pencil venture was pretty typical, I think, in that I always tried to find out what people needed that they weren't getting. And then I'd pull together the experts who could fill the gap.

When prohibition was repealed in the US, for example, I saw the need for barrels to put beer in and for staves to make the barrels. So I got into that business. And from there, I got into the whiskey business. We couldn't use grain, because it was needed during the war. But there was a potato surplus, and we were able to convert potatoes to make alcohol which we could use to blend with aged whiskey.

Your ability to spot unfulfilled needs goes a long way toward explaining the success of your operations once they're established, Dr. Hammer. But why do you think you've been so successful in establishing yourself in what other corporate people have regarded as impossible political environments abroad? You've dealt with everybody from Lenin and Brezhnev to Colonel Qaddafi of Libya. And you've prospered under nationalists and regimes of the right and left. What's the key?

Well, I'm an old farmer. And I remember that you can't get anything out of the soil until you've put something in. If you don't fertilize, you won't get a good crop and your land will soon be worthless.

That same applies to countries. We can't just pump out profits and have them feel we're exploiting them. It's all right for us to want to make a legitimate return on our enterprise, but we should also demonstrate interest in the welfare of the countries where we operate. We should be willing to find out their needs and to reinvest profits there.

Particularly in dealing with foreign governments, also, I think it's very important that a chief executive not delegate too much authority. A man becomes chief executive because he has shown ability, industry and a willingness to dedicate himself to his work. He should go personally to see what's going on in every place where his company operates. Too many chief executives fail to do that.

But you do?

Yes. I've made it my business to visit every branch of our company. There's hardly any manager or division that I haven't visited. And the same applies to countries where we work. I try to meet the head of state wherever I can. And then I filter down and meet people in the lower echelons, too. I try to know them, to find out what their problems are.

A year after the Libyan revolution, for example, I heard that the country was going to nationalize an oil company, and I was told that it might be us. This was an important crisis—our biggest oil operation is in Libya—and I wasn't about to send subordinates. I flew there immediately and was met by Colonel Jaloud, then Prime Minister. He said, "You're the first oil company chief executive who has come to see us since the revolution." All the major oil firms operate in Libya and, not one had sent its chief executive!

Why do you think?

It was a lack of perception, a failure to understand that you can accomplish more face-to-face. You can write a lot of letters, you can delegate authority and send subordinates. But if you don't go yourself, you don't get or give the same impression.

When you went to Libya, how did you resolve the nationalization threat?

Well, there was a dispute at the time about the tax they were getting, and they wanted a 25 cent-a-barrel increase. It was a piddling amount, and yet the major oil companies had refused to accede.

You disagreed with the other companies?

I thought they were being foolish. The Libyans knew what profits the major oil companies were making. For them to not meet the Libyans halfway, I felt, was a mistake.

What did you do?

We went along with the increase. A few years later, we agreed to sell the Libyans 51 percent of our enterprise. We were the first to do that.

You took this action voluntarily?

That's right. You know, we've always reasoned that, if we could create contracts that fit the nationalist aspirations of the host countries, we could avoid the spectre of nationalization.

Has your Libyan experience borne out that philosophy?

Absolutely. Our deal pleased the Libyans, because it gave them a sense that they had a majority control of their own resources. Now they have no desire to take over the other 49 percent. Because they've seen how well the present arrangement works. They have our cooperation, our management and our technical skills.

Meanwhile, we have the right to buy back and market the 51 percent government share of the oil, which is a unique feature in this sort of arrangement. And because of certain clauses in our long-term contracts, we're able to increase our production and make as much money out of our 49 percent as we did when we had 100 percent. We're also more popular with the Libyan government than at any previous time during the ten years we've been there. So it works out well.

If other companies had followed the same course, we might have avoided the situation we're in today. But they didn't, and now the oil producing countries have gotten together under OPEC and gotten the western world very worried. Because the price of oil is going up.

Venezuela, as you know, has purchased the entire interests of all foreign oil companies and made service contracts with them to market the oil. Do you think we'll be seeing more of that sort of thing, Dr. Hammer?

I can't say for sure. But I think a country's making a mistake when they buy 100 percent of a foreign company's enterprise. I think they'd be much better off if they had, say, 51 percent. Because it's to their advantage to keep the companies interested in making new oil discoveries and capital investments. If the investor gets a fair return on his enterprise, he'll invest money in the country. And he'll gradually teach the local people to become geologists and engineers.

Would you advise a US company to go into countries that are either moving toward nationalization or making 51 percent/49 percent deals? Or would you tell them that there are better places to put capital?

Right now, I think the best place to put capital is in the United States. There's plenty of room for investment right here.

Do Occidental's investments reflect that belief?

Oh, yes. Coal is this country's most important remaining natural resource, so we're increasing our investment in that. After coal, I think chemical companies are going to be getting a large part of our capital. And in oil, we're bidding on and being awarded a number of off-shore drilling leases. We're very enthusiastic about that.

Last but not least, there's our Colorado shale oil, which we think is the greatest hope of all. We have a film, "Why Move the Mountain?," which tells the whole story. It explains why we think our process of extracting shale oil *in situ* is the only viable one from an environmental standpoint. We think there's a great future in it.

At the same time, you certainly haven't turned your back on international markets. You signed a deal with the Russians that is called the largest commercial venture to date between the two nations.

That's correct. We estimate the value of the deal, over a 20-year period, at $20 billion.

We will ship phosphates, of which the US has a surplus, and the Soviets will send us ammonia and urea made from natural gas, which are in short supply in America. The agreement also covers natural gas, metal-finishing, solid-waste disposal and the building of an international trade center in Moscow.

Oxy's deal strikes me as particularly impressive because trade relations have generally cooled between the US and Russia over the past few years. How did your agreement originate?

I was invited to Moscow by the Russian government in 1972. I went on a fact-finding mission with a whole team of our executives. And after I was there a week, the Russians presented us with the draft of a trade agreement. It was extraordinary, because trade agreements are usually made between countries. This was the first time that the Russians had offered such a deal to a private company.

Well, I read the document through and it sounded fine to me. So I crossed out the word "draft," signed it and handed it back.

Just like that?

Yes. They were quite taken aback and they said, "Don't you want to show it to your lawyers?" I told them it looked fair and workable and that I didn't need my lawyers. Then I handed them the pen. And after a few minutes, they signed. That was the beginning of the present arrangement.

Being head of a public company, then, has not impeded your ability to make quick decisions?

No, it hasn't changed my style. I did the same thing when I met with the Libyans. I thought their requests were fair and I sat down and told them so. Right on the spot.

Had you discussed the Libyan decision with your board of directors beforehand? Or did you tell them after the fact?

Before I left for Libya, we knew the problem. And the Board agreed to trust my judgment.

I find that, if you have a board of directors composed of capable, independent and intelligent men, you won't have a problem. If you're able to convince them of the correctness of your views, they'll go along with you. We've never had a divided vote on our board.

Let me ask you about a related area. As Chief Executive Officer of Occidental, Dr. Hammer, you've been involved with overall strategy planning. And Joseph Baird, the Chief Operating Officer, concentrates on day-to-day activities. But how exactly do you draw the line between your responsibilities?

Well, I keep out of operations and let him handle that. But our work is very interrelated, of course, so we stay in very close touch. I sit in all policy talks and he discusses all important matters with me. Every day, also, we're either on the telephone or we meet for a little while.

Then, once a month, we have a two-day management meeting where all executives come. He sits through them and I just come in for a wrap-up on the second day. So I keep in touch with what's going on. And I still have time to travel, to meet people and to conduct high-level negotiations.

On a major decision, such as whether or not to invest in some new coal mines, what would your role be? And what role would the chief operating officer play?

Our staff would have to prepare an AFE (Authority for Expenditure) report and come before the executive committee or board of directors to justify the cost. I'm chairman of both committees, so that I'd be aware of any request for capital in excess of a million dollars. But once we'd made the decision to go ahead, the execution would be in the hands of Mr. Baird. I'd concentrate more on the long-term picture.

Based on your massive experience, Dr. Hammer, how do you view that picture? What do you see as the responsibility of senior management in terms of dealing with today's world?

Well, the first responsibility of top management is to maintain the present private enterprise system which has given our people the best standard of living of any country in the world.

If we are to perpetuate that system, we have to take our responsibilities seriously, and we have to see that inequities are corrected. We also have to find a way to avoid the terrible ups and downs that we have in our economy. Otherwise, we'll risk losing out to the socialist system.

When you say "socialist," do you include Russia?

Yes, because I feel that Russia is socialist rather than communist. Communism is something that Karl Marx may have spoken about. But I think Lenin modified it when he developed his New Economic Policy in 1921. I had conversations with him about it, and I'm convinced that that was the turning point. The Russians today haven't given up on communism as an eventual goal, I think, but they feel that socialism is the way to reach it.

In any case, various forms of socialism exist now all over the world. And this is the competition for our so-called capitalist system. I don't think "capitalist" is the right word for it anymore, because there are tens of millions of stockholders in the US, and I'm sure you couldn't properly call all of them "capitalists."

Having dealt with the Russians for half a century, do you feel that their system offers any advantages over ours?

They have no unemployment, and that's important. Because every man who's willing to work should have a job and a means of supporting his family. I think it's a disgrace that, under our system, there's any unemployment at all if people are willing to work. The fear of losing a job and being put on relief is demoralizing. And business executives must find a way to create jobs and employ as many people as possible.

Well, you've certainly demonstrated your own ability to find needs to fill and create jobs. How many have you created at Occidental alone?

About 33,000. But I believe that business by itself cannot solve the unemployment problem. Government must do more. We may have to support full employment by public works, but that doesn't necessarily mean we have to have more taxation. We might already have enough taxes to do the job—if only our government were properly managed.

What's wrong with government from this standpoint?

We've left the running of government to politicians. It needs more participation by businessmen, who know what it means to face a payroll and who know how to run an operation economically.

While we're discussing government, Dr. Hammer, I'd like to ask you a little about Watergate. It's been said that everyone Nixon touched, particularly in the business community, was hurt. I've heard people say that he posed as a friend of business but that, detente aside, he really did business more harm than good. How do you react to that? I'm not talking about the specifics of what you personally went through, but about the general impact on business of the Nixon era, the Watergate mentality.

Well, I think that, in a way, Watergate has been a good thing for this country. Because business has begun to realize that it can no longer operate the way it had.

Some foreign companies, I suppose, will continue to use payoffs. American manufacturers will have difficulty competing with them, but we'll have to rely on the efficiency of our equipment and services which are in fact superior. We'll also have to draw up marketing methods which will enable us to compete better.

And eventually, I hope, foreign and American companies will get together on a standard of morality that will discourage any possibility of paying off to a foreign government. I think the world is changing. And business is going to have to change with it.

T. Mitchell Ford

Chairman of the Board and President and Chief Executive Officer
Emhart Corporation

Pick any major point in the world's marketplace, and chances are Emhart Corporation is represented. The firm employs 33,000 people in 30 countries. Its annual revenues now exceed $1 billion.

Emhart products are grouped in six major fields: construction, foods and beverages, packaging, rubber and plastics, shoes, and transportation. The consumer is unlikely to recognize the Emhart name, for only one-third of its products, such as Kwikset hardware and door locks, are sold to the consumer.

But industry knows Emhart well. Its bottle-making machinery is in demand worldwide. Its injection molders find wide application in the plastics industry; its rubber-making machines in the tire indus-

try. In the shoe industry, its USM Corporation (formerly United Shoe Machinery) is the leader in tanning and cutting machinery as well as in shoe manufacturing equipment. It is a major factor in industrial chemicals, in metal fasteners and in supermarket food merchandising units.

Given these impressive facts and figures, one might expect to find Emhart headquartered in a large Manhattan office and chaired by a rather formal-mannered person. But the firm is run out of a modest-sized, unpretentious building in a rural Farmington, Connecticut. And the affable man at the top, who joined the company in 1958, evidences a decidedly informal management style.

He is T. Mitchell Ford, an attorney, and Emhart's president and chief executive officer since 1967. Earlier, he served as general counsel to the Naugatuck Valley [Connecticut] Industrial Council and as an attorney and assistant general counsel to the Central Intelligence Agency in Washington, D.C.

What strikes me first, Mike, is the size and location of your headquarters. Yours is a billion-dollar, multinational corporation; yet you operate from a relatively small building in a rural area of Connecticut. That seems to say something about your value system and style of management.

Well, we've always regarded Emhart Corporation and the products we manufacture as being relatively mundane. We sell basic-type products and mostly just to industrial customers. I guess that has something to do with it.

Our previous headquarters building, though, wasn't anything like this. It won an architectural award and was three times the size of this one.

Why did you move?

Looking out at a hundred acres of lawn, I got to thinking that perhaps we could use the money better in the business. So we sold the old building for about $9 million, used the proceeds in part to buy the stock of USM, and moved in here. All we really needed was a place that's comfortable to work in. This place is.

That being the case, you must have a very small headquarters staff for a firm of your size.

We have about 85 people here, but I don't know what constitutes a "small" headquarters staff. We have what we need here: the legal department, the financial department, the human resources people, public affairs and public relations.

Do you also have computer terminals to help you collect data from your various plant locations?

No, we don't. We do have a gentleman here who monitors expenditures and operations in the EDP area of our operating groups. But we feel that we should be a little cautious about leaping forward in the computer area. We've found that we can make steady progress by having someone monitor the cost/benefit ratio of our systems.

But figures can't tell you the whole story. How do you dig beneath them to find out what's really going on at your various plants and divisions?

Our system, if you can call it that, has historically been to get behind the numbers by making personal visits to our people. Customarily, we go to the divisions early each year, when we're doing what we call our business review. And we visit them again toward the end of the year when we're preparing new budgets. So twice a year, we're on the scene, walking through the plants, probing into the business and talking with the people.

Do you personally make any of these visits?

Oh, yes, quite frequently. What I've tried to do, particularly since our merger with USM, is to get out to all the locations, even the smaller ones. Because I believe it's important to the guy in the little plant at the end of the line to know that people in the upper echelons care what happens to him. Also, if he has something on his mind, it gives him the opportunity to get it out.

Might he be a little bit in awe of the chairman?

Perhaps at first. But I'll take a little walk through the plant and maybe sit down and have a cup of coffee with the people. By that time, things get pretty loose. The result is that top management here knows about the company's operations in depth: plant conditions, housekeeping as well as the hopes and fears of the individuals involved.

Do the operating heads accompany you on these visits?

Well, if they can't come, I'll go anyway. But I always invite them and, whenever possible, they're there with me.

I've just finished ten days in Europe with Herbert Jarvis, USM's president, for example. We went to review USM's research and development programs. And I had a wonderful chance to see not only their new products, but also their management methods and so on.

Tell me a little about this trip, Mike.

We went to Frankfurt to see USM's shoe-machinery operation. We also took a look at their Bostik Chemical Group. Then we went to Birmingham, England, where the USM Fastener Group has a large plant, and to Leicester, to review USM's British United Machinery Group.

At that point, Mr. Jarvis went home. But I remembered a little Emhart operation about 50 miles away, in Doncaster, and decided to stick around. I hadn't been there in about three years, and thought I might fit in a visit while I was so close. So I went there. And, that same day, I stopped by a USM machinery plant in Rochdale which I'd not previously visited. After that, I flew to Amsterdam, met Emhart Industries President Bill Lichtenfels, and went to see VSB, our Dutch hardware company.

That's quite an itinerary.

Yes, it's a very busy series of one-night stands. But I know of no other way to do it, and I'm convinced that it has to be done.

Consider my visit to Emhart U.K. in Doncaster, where I talked to the fellow who heads that operation. I've known him for years but, until this visit, I hadn't seen him since he'd become general manager at Doncaster. So we had dinner and went through the plant together. And he was understandably very anxious to show me what he'd done. I also got to take a look at a prototype machine his research and development people had come up with. And I had lunch in the plant cafeteria—the cook there baked me a cake—and made a speech and took questions.

What sorts of questions were you asked?

Oh, they wanted to know about USM operations in the area. A lot of Emhart people, myself included, really don't know enough about USM and vice versa. Which is why I'm now emphasizing USM locations when I travel. I'm trying to find out in depth how they do their business.

I've just read an article about a company chief who apparently visits his operating people as often as you do. His form of "hands-on" management involves long, formal grillings of his managers. Is that your style?

No, it's not. I don't come on that strong, and I don't try to intimidate people. I simply try to get to the locations regularly and to use my visits to find out how the business has been doing. I want to see what people can tell me and I also want to act as a sounding board for their questions.

You've said that your operating heads sometimes accompany you on these visits. What about Emhart's directors? Do you ever bring them along?

Yes, I do. I want our directors to see every single plant I can get them to. In 1972 or 1973, we took our whole board to Sweden, where we have a big investment. After the USM merger in 1976, we took the board to Boston, where USM has been headquartered. I'm taking them to England, to see our large operation there, very shortly. After the U.K. meeting, also, many of our directors will be going on to the Continent. We've asked those people to stop in at plants near where they'll be traveling.

Why did you consider it so important for your directors to make these visits?

The more plants they've seen, as a general rule, the better directors they are. They relate to the business, because they have mental pictures of its operations. Also, they've met the management. If someone comes up for a promotion, they can say, "Oh, I remember that fellow. I met him at such-and-such a plant."

Okay. Now, aside from the plant visits, how do you and the board determine what's really going on out in the field?
Well, we have the usual financial reports, which are prepared monthly. Every month, we have a Board of Directors meeting where we hear from finance as well as from our two operating heads.

Every month? That's a bit unusual, isn't it?
Yes, sir.

Is the board composed mostly of outsiders?
Yes, and I personally believe that it should be that way. On the other hand, we do have a higher proportion of inside directors than we've historically had. But it's a very strong board in my opinion. Very supportive, yet quite inquisitive. Very much a bunch of individuals.

So they're a valuable source of input?
Yes. In addition, I get good input from my operating heads.
I might add that it's been my experience that close physical association with the operating heads can help give you the real flavor of the business. Mr. Lichtenfels, for example, is located in this building. And we're now in the process of moving the Boston office of USM here, too. We're taking its staff services—legal, financial, industrial relations, manufacturing—and consolidating them at the Emhart corporate level. As part of this, Mr. Jarvis of USM is moving here. And I think it will be a great help to both of us to be physically located in the same building.
You know, the doors are open around this place and we all have a tendency to go in and out—which is just the way I want it. If I see a number on a financial report, for example, it's very easy for me to just walk down the hall to Bill Lichtenfels' office and say, "I notice this is happening. What does it mean?"

But how do you know what figures to question?
Partly by trying to stay in businesses with which I have some degree of

familiarity. I've been exposed to the businesses we deal in for something more than fifteen years now. I think I have some idea, for example, of where you might expect variations to appear in a financial report on one of those businesses.

Do you lean heavily on your financial department for information?
Yes, because we believe strongly in controls and in the credibility of numbers. We like to know on a continuing basis how much cash we've got. And we like to be assured that, when we've got a number, it's a good number. I leave discussion of the numbers to the experts. If you read our analyst presentations, you'll find that my part of the thing covers trends and so forth. I myself don't hand out any numbers to the public for our company.

How often do you receive financial input on your various operations?
Well, from Emhart Industries, I expect a statement on the ninth day after the end of each month. Some of it comes in by phone, but the bulk arrives by mail or teletype. What I see first is not a balance sheet, but raw, usually handwritten data on earnings. It will show month and year and comparisons with the previous year and the current budget.

Does USM also submit such data on the ninth of each month?
We're having difficulty with USM on this, because they're not used to producing information with the degree of timeliness we require. One problem is that they have an awful lot of small operations where one person might simultaneously serve as bookkeeper, controller and purchasing agent. Also, USM operates in some very faraway places: Australia, New Zealand and the like.
We're thinking of using satellite transmissions to speed up data-gathering from places like that. And, as I've said, USM's headquarters is moving here. That should also make for faster reporting.

What is the practical value of being able to have this information so quickly? Have there been instances when its timely arrival has allowed you to deal with trouble spots more rapidly than you otherwise might?
One incident in particular comes to mind. In one of our businesses, there's a very large, dominant customer whom everybody in the industry watches. The idea is that, if you get a cancellation from them, there may be some more cancellations coming in behind it from smaller companies in the industry.

Well, almost five years ago, I spotted a fall-off in orders and called up the head of the appropriate Emhart division to find out where the cancellations were coming from. It turned out that the customer I've mentioned had withdrawn several orders with us for machines that run over $500,000 each.

Was your division manager as aware of the significance of this as you were?

Probably, but I think the fact that I was raising questions might have forced him to pay a little more attention to the situation than he might otherwise have done. You know, I don't want to tell a division manager how to run his business. But I can certainly say, "From where I'm sitting, this could be trouble."

In this case, how did the division man react?

He said we'd better watch out or we might wind up with excess inventory. The machinery we're talking about is put together on a very long-lead basis and a lot of the parts for it are subcontracted. So he began checking his purchase orders for subcontracted materials. And he did what he could to make adjustments.

So this was a situation where the prompt receipt of data played a key role for you.

Well, we were at least aware that a problem might be developing. So we had time to react.

Okay, Mike. You've talked about internal financial information and about the visits to your various plants. Where else do you get data? You must watch national social and economic trends.

We watch them. But most of that information-gathering is done at the various operating divisions. They're the experts on their industries. We don't employ a resident economist.

As for internal data, when I said we do a business review early in the year and a budget review at the tail end, I forgot one other thing: that in the middle of the year, we have what we call a "divisional presidents' meeting." Those last about three days and cover a wide number of areas. So I get a total of three big "shots" a year with regard to the condition of our industries. I also read a lot: *Fortune, Business Week, Forbes,* the usual assortment of business magazines.

What about your membership on outside boards? Do those involvements also teach you things that you can apply to Emhart?

They're very rewarding because I have the opportunity to see how other companies manage the same types of problems that I have to resolve. In one company where I'm a director, for example, I observed a method of handling inventory control which I thought was very well done. We modified it slightly and have tried to install it in some of our divisions. As a director of another company, I encountered what I regarded to be a very good set of forms for management development. So I just grabbed all the paper, brought it over here, and asked permission to let our people see it. Through my work on still another board, I became familiar with what I'd call a very sophisticated, formal, long-range planning technique. That really interested me, because we don't have anything so detailed. I want to keep my eye on the mechanics of how it might be done.

All in all, you seem to be keeping your eye on a quite a lot of things. How do you find the time?

One of the incidental by-products of the plant visits is that I spend a lot of time on airplanes. And that gives me an opportunity to catch up on reading and thinking.

Also, we have a number of people at the Emhart staff level to whom I have a tendency to delegate authority. They're people I've worked with for years, people I'm very comfortable with who I believe are also quite comfortable with my style of doing things. Without them, this place would be a mess. But when they do their jobs, I can go off and do my job and have some time to think.

How many staff people are we talking about now?

I try to have no more than six people reporting directly to me. Under the structure I'm contemplating now, they would include Mr. Jarvis and Mr. Lichtenfels—the two operating heads—plus the heads of our financial, administrative and legal areas. And perhaps John Budd, our Vice President for Public Relations. So, five or six people.

From what you've said, I gather you work on a very informal basis with this group. But what's the atmosphere when you hold meetings that include other staff?

Well, at each business review meeting, we do normally have formal presentations. But the content of those presentations would depend on the individual. We don't have a standard corporate way of reporting at these meetings. We may at some point, but we don't now.

In any case, though, you're describing a businesslike atmosphere rather than an intimidatory one?

Oh, definitely. We're not there to beat up people. My experience is that that would only make them hesitant to be fully truthful.

What we want at our meetings is two-way conversation. We have reports from manufacturing, sales, research, finance, and the people end of the business. The fellows who run these operations each get up and make a presentation, and we discuss and question. Hopefully, by the end of the meeting we'll have gotten into all the nooks and crannies of the business.

All right. We've been discussing your management style as it relates to information-gathering. How much attention do you pay to sending information out of the chairman's office? Is there a steady stream of Ford memos?

No. In fact, there aren't any I can think of on a regular basis. We use an in-house newspaper as a communications device, but there's no Ford column in there. We reprint my speeches and that sort of thing. But in general, I communicate in written form quite rarely with the operating people.

Why?

Mr. Jarvis, I guess, communicates with his people in writing. So does Mr. Lichtenfels. And I don't want anyone to think I'm trying to bypass them. That would cut the legs out from under them.

Besides, my style is more informal. I'd rather communicate through my visits to the operating locations. When I get a chance to travel and give little talks to the people, I always include some observations about what we tried to do in the previous year and what we're attempting currently.

How much time do you spend communicating to people outside the company? Business and community groups? The government?

We do not have a large governmental exposure. As for trade associations and this sort of thing, I try to do our share, but most of Emhart's participation is at the divisional level. And Mr. Brewster, our Vice Chairman, represents us at things like the Business Council, the Conference Board and Business International. As for me, I frankly feel that my first responsibility now is to the business. When that calms down, perhaps I'll have more time for outside activity.

How do you view Emhart's responsibility to the communities where you operate?

Well, we have maybe thirty plant locations in the US, and there's a community responsibility at every one of them. We've analyzed all our plants for environmental standards and pollution hazards and are making necessary changes. When we merged with USM, we created a "Social Responsibility Committee" within our board of directors. And we're now giving out roughly half a million dollars a year to various charities. That's a lot of money. We've put in a scholarship program for our employees, and a tuition-refund program. That sort of thing.

But I've had a lingering question for many years as to whether we're doing a good job in this area. Are we throwing money on things just because, historically, this is where industry has thrown money? Should we be examining our contributions program more carefully? Should we be spending more? Or less? Or on something different?

Have past mistakes prompted these questions?

To a large extent. For example, we and some of the other businesses around Hartford poured millions a few years ago into trying to devise a plan for a "perfect" city. We hired consultants, who selected a little town for the project, and we bought up quite a bit of acreage there. Well, the town felt that the smart alecks in Hartford were trying to run their lives. Nobody had taken into account how they might feel. And the whole project just bombed. We also spent a great deal of money trying to find a better way to deliver health care. And over the years, one part after another of that study was simply dropped. So now we're asking questions about where we can most effectively put our charitable contributions.

How exactly have the bad experiences you've described affected your feelings about what business can do in the area of social responsibility?

One thing it's proved to me is that, while business can make a contribution, it should make it in areas where it has some degree of expertise. I think some of the industrial and commercial companies around here have people whose talents can be used for community benefit. I think we can supply money, too, as long as we're more careful about how we spend it than we have been in the past. We've got to weigh cost versus benefit.

I might add that, on the subject of minorities, we ought to be more willing to take risks than we might be with some other things. And I think Emhart has done that.

Have you been involved with the Urban League here?

Yes, we have, and on a highly credible basis. They know we're not participating just for the fun and games.

What social responsibilities do you think business should not assume? In setting up a corporate community program, what lines would you draw?

Mainly, I'm just saying that business ought not to try to pour money on everything. Corporations can get people running all over the place. In other words, I wouldn't do that "perfect city" experiment three or four times. I think we should learn our lesson, and pay more attention to making sure our contributions are meaningful.

Also, I wouldn't make social involvement a condition of employment for our managers. If they're not committed, don't force them. I'm fascinated with Xerox, where they give people sabbaticals to work in the community. You know, I wonder what those sabbaticals do to a guy's career. He comes back in six months and perhaps the corporation went that-a-way. Similar problems can develop with a chief executive officer. I've seen situations where they got so involved with community affairs that the company started to go down the drain.

So I think you can go overboard. We should make it possible for people at Emhart to work in the community. But I think they should go in with their eyes open. And they shouldn't be led to believe that career advancement will depend on how much they do outside.

With those reservations, Mike, what sorts of community projects would you like to see Emhart become more involved in?

I personally think the place to start is education. If we can improve the educational process for some of our minorities, we'll be a long way towards solving the minorities' problems. And I'm hopeful that it can be done.

Do you find educators willing to listen and learn from business?

I haven't gotten into much of a one-on-one conversation with an educator. I hope to soon, though, because the guy who runs Emhart's scholarship program is an old classmate of mine who's now running a boys' preparatory school. I want to try out some of my theories on him.

Let's get back to the business of Emhart, because I want to talk a little about your research and development operations. Last week, I bought one of your "911" smoke detectors, and was very highly impressed. It's extremely sophisticated. It works perfectly. And it really does install in five minutes. Did that require a lot of R&D? Did the operating people come to management to solicit money to develop it? What was the procedure?

My recollection is that the origins of the smoke detector are completely at variance with the normal way we invent things here. Back when Mr. Lichtenfels was in the hardware end of the business, he decided on his own that there might be a wonderful future in battery-operated smoke detectors for the residential market. He made a list of the features he felt such a device should contain, and he calculated the price he thought a saleable detector could not exceed. He handed all that to our R&D people at corporate headquarters and they, in effect, invented the device to his specifications.

Why is this so at variance with the way you generally invent things?

Well, for one thing, we no longer do any research and development at corporate headquarters. We've broken it up and pushed it into the divisions, because I felt there'd be a much more fruitful R&D effort if it took place closer to the actual operations. You know, the operating divisions have a tendency to distrust anything they don't invent, particularly if it comes out of headquarters 3,000 miles away.

As Emhart has grown, have you found it necessary to break up other functions as well?

Yes.

We used to double up on a lot of jobs. Our internal public relations, for example, was run by the man who was also in charge of our industrial relations and people. Our treasurer, when he wasn't doing something else, ran our pension administration and investment program.

Well, when we acquired USM, it occurred to me that somewhere between $350 million and a billion, you reach a size where you can't have an individual doing two or three things. Because each job becomes more consuming and requires more specialization.

As a result, we're planning more staff services. An insurance guy who does nothing but. A pension guy who devotes all his time to that. All in all, we may add 30 people. We're at a size now where we can afford it.

I'm sure the company's growth has had a large impact on the nature of your own job. But you seem to have things very much under control. Your desk isn't buried in paper. And you don't seem pressured.

Well, anybody gets pressure. But this place is set up so that, if everybody's doing what he should, my job is maybe to sit and do some thinking. I have to spend a lot of time thinking about the type of company we're building and the type we want to build. And I'm very aware of the perils of growing too fast and getting corporate indigestion as a result. So I like to work deliberately and carefully, with a minimum of pressure, so I can be very sure that we know what we're doing.

As for the desk, I guess I'm just a clean-desk type of person: I have a tendency to send the paper somewhere. And you can always tell when my desk gets nice and clean, because I start wandering around the office talking to people.

How much of your communicating with senior staff takes place on those strolls?

Quite a lot of it. We don't have as many formal meetings as other companies. And though we used to have a lot of committees, we haven't got any right now. Everybody's just in and out.

When we do have meetings, also, they tend to be as impromptu as my walks. After I came back here from Europe last week, for example, a woman on the first floor stopped me going in the door. She said, "We ought to have a meeting on the USM move from Boston to Farmington. We've got people who have questions." I said "Fine," and that's what we did. We did it in three sessions, because we included everyone—the janitor, the secretaries, everyone—and the board room couldn't fit them all at once.

I think all of what you've been saying reflects a very distinctive management style, Mike. Do you think it's a function of your personality? Or is it something you've consciously developed because you feel informal communications are most effective?

I'm sure any chief executive's style results partly because it's the one he's most comfortable with. But I think my style also relates to the company's origins. We've grown very fast, but we were a small company not all that long ago. We've always been headquartered in a little town and lived in the neighborhood. The members of the top management group are personal friends. And really, we're a bunch of country boys. That's an oversimplification, but there's a lot of truth to it.

Richard R. Shinn

President and Chief Executive Officer
Metropolitan Life Insurance Company

In a narrow sense, Richard Shinn's position has not changed since the late thirties, when he graduated from New Jersey's Rider College and landed his first job at Metropolitan Life's New York headquarters. He has been with Metropolitan ever since, and has, in fact, spent his entire career at One Madison Avenue, the company's home office.

His roles and responsibilities have changed, and quite dramatically. Starting with Metropolitan as a $15-a-week mailboy, he soon won an assignment to the firm's rapidly expanding group insurance department. Constantly striving to improve his knowledge of a complex business, he took almost every insurance course that Metropolitan and the insurance industry offered, and earned promotions in rapid succession. Two years after being named to a vice presidency and the top spot in the group department, he was appointed to di-

rect Metropolitan's corporate planning efforts. He became president of the company and a director in 1969, and in 1973 assumed the additional title of chief executive officer.

To grasp the enormity of Shinn's current responsibilities, consider that Metropolitan, one of the largest corporations in America, insures over 46 million people—or about one of every five men, women and children in the US and Canada. It has $37.5 billion in assets, more than 50,000 employees, and approximately 1,000 North American offices.

Directing such a vast organization obviously requires long hours of work. But Shinn, a father of three and an avid golfer, finds time for a wide array of outside activities. Deeply involved with helping to solve the problems of New York City, he was one of a four-man panel appointed by New York Governor Hugh Carey that was responsible for the creation of "Big MAC," the Municipal Assistance Corporation. He chairs the Mayor's Management Advisory Board, which has developed programs to greatly improve the City's management procedures, and was a member of the Mayor's Temporary Commission on City Finances. A board member of the Economic Development Council, the New York Chamber of Commerce and Industry and the United Fund of Greater New York, Shinn also serves on the boards of a number of corporations, as a trustee of several universities, and is immediate past chairman of the American Council of Life Insurance, his industry's largest and most prestigious association.

Unlike most of your predecessors as chief executive officer, you're not a specialist in any particular area of the business. Would that be a fair statement?

Yes, it would. There have been attorneys in my job, actuaries and financial experts. But I think of myself as being more of a generalist. I'm not a financial man, or a lawyer or an actuary. I've never been out in the hinterlands selling either, but there are times I wish I had because marketing is so vital to our business.

You must have seen quite a variety of management styles over the years. Have you developed a style of your own?

I'm not sure that one's management style is methodically and carefully developed as though you were designing a house. I think a management style tends to reflect the personality of the individual. It is influenced, in part, by associates with whom you are working, and how the company is organized. I think it is also tied in with what the company's priorities are and what is going on in the marketplace as well as in government.

If I had to describe my management style I think I would use the word "participation." I want as much participation from my associates in the decision-making process as possible. I want them to feel that when decisions are made, they are implementing programs which they had a part in developing.

I liken my role as chief executive to that of the conductor of a symphony orchestra. First, you are responsible for selecting the players. You don't pretend that you are more expert than each of the musicians in the orchestra, but you must have the knack of identifying those who can make the best contribution to the orchestra. Next, you set the standards against which performance is going to be measured. Third, you select the program, the various musical pieces the orchestra is to play. This is the planning role. And finally, you must bring this group of individual experts together so that the entire performance produces the kind of music you want without projecting the feeling that each musician must identify himself apart from the orchestra as a whole.

Management style, then, involves the whole question of leadership—how you inspire and how you provide an environment where your associates are likely to be self-motivated; how you lay out plans, priorities and objectives; how you set standards; how you work with your associates; how you organize your time. And finally, how you get all of this together so that, in the final analysis, everyone has the feeling of participating in the sense that the conductor and the players participate in an orchestra—in a unified way, as one.

Following the analogy, you play some instruments pretty well yourself. How do you resist getting involved with those areas with which you are particularly familiar?

That's one of the restraints I must exercise. I must confess, it's an eternal struggle. I must keep remembering that it's my job to be the conductor—that I should not try to be the first violinist or the oboe player or the tympanist. Chief executives who have been activists—that is, who have been deeply involved with others in the day-to-day operations of the company—find it difficult to stay on the podium where they belong. I know I do. I'm mixing my metaphors here, but it is like being a football coach, too. He must stay on the sidelines, he can't get out on the field and be the quarterback, or the tackle, or the end. He must depend on the players to do the job assigned to them.

The decision-making process. Is this a formal process? Do you feel it is instinctive, intuitive? What is your own approach?

Decision-making is a many-splendored thing. There are those decisions that must be made quickly, on occasion even before all the facts are in. In these instances, decisions are part intuition, part experience and part reliance on those who are advising you. Then there are the more fundamental decisions that require a more structured approach.

The first step toward making good decisions is getting reliable, timely, well-considered information. Once you have high-quality input, many decisions practically make themselves. Pertinent facts lead inevitably in a certain direction. The question is, how inclusive are the facts at hand. Very often I find that differences of opinions arise among my associates because they are working from different or incomplete sets of facts. When this happens it takes longer to achieve a consensus. So an initial agreement on the basic facts is a necessary goal in decision-making.

There is one thing I find indispensable when someone makes a very important or fundamental recommendation: that the recommendation not only include supporting documents for the suggested decision, but the rejected alternatives as well. With all of this information in hand I find that I am evaluating the entire situation more confidently. When a decision is made, then I know nothing has been overlooked, or left out, or not given proper weight.

On occasion my associates feel this pro and con approach is unnecessary—that I should rely largely upon their recommendations alone. I think, however, I have a responsibility to take the more inclusive approach.

Do you, in the decision-making process, find that you have a different approach for different kinds of decisions, that is, people decisions as opposed to dollar decisions, for instance?

The answer has to be yes. Decisions involving people or company organization, for example, often have to be very subjective. They are not liable to precise measurement. Judgmental factors come into play in a more substantial way than when you deal solely with established facts.

It's clear that you believe in sharing the load, in moving decision-making down the line. It's also clear that you want to push your company very hard. How do you motivate people to work together as aggressively and effectively as you yourself work?

At Metropolitan we have what we call the Corporate Executive Office. This consists of the chief executive, the chairman of the board, and the senior officers of our major departments—six of us in all. Each member of the Corporate Executive Office is charged with considering the company as a whole as opposed to from the single vantage point of his respective department. The philosophy behind this high-level unit is, in a word, complete involvement. The major components of Metropolitan, through the Corporate Executive Office, become part and parcel of the entire operation. They become a vital two-way communications link, and information concerning the company as a whole is disseminated with greater facility and accuracy.

With this office, the company can benefit from the expertise of its senior management in all areas, not just specialized areas. We meet periodically to review overall company operations and discuss results. And believe me, everyone makes a contribution at these meetings. The Corporate Executive Office has been an effective vehicle for Metropolitan in these times of dramatic change. We work hard, and I think it's because basically we all want the same things. If I were trying to get people to enthusiastically support programs simply because I think they're right, it would be very difficult. But if we together, the senior people, recognize the things we all want, and if each of us understands his role in achieving them, we don't have a constant need for aggressive persuasion. And I think we do have a group that is as anxious to get where we need to go as I am. They're all self-motivated.

But aren't self-motivated people apt to be very independent in their thinking?

Sure, they all have great pride and conviction in their own ideas. I'd be disappointed if they didn't. But it goes back to my analogy of the orchestra leader. You have to get all these people to want to be part of the total effort. I think we're making progress toward that end. But frankly, I think we have a way to go toward bringing about the cohesiveness that we need. As I've said, the top people here are all self-motivated. Getting them to blend together is the challenge.

Still, you seem to value their individuality and self-motivation.

Good executives have to be self-motivated along with having integrity, professional skills, and all that. But first, they have to be self-motivated, and, I might add, highly competitive. I'm talking about the type of person who doesn't like to lose at golf or anything else, who really enjoys winning. That person will use the tools we have better than another person will.

You know, we just promoted a young fellow to a very senior position in our marketing operation, and we've analyzed just why he was so successful so early in his career. We learned, first of all, that he utilized our management tools and set high standards for himself and those under him. But most important, he liked people and they liked him and met his standards. In other words, he could be demanding and still be friendly, which isn't easy. Of equal importance, he really enjoyed running things. I think the executive is an individual who wants the authority to hold the reins. And he, or she, wants the recognition that goes with success. With this in mind, consider that our experience has shown that an average manager, for example, in an excellent sales territory will get average results, while an outstanding manager in an average territory will get outstanding results. So, to a large extent, an operation will rise or fall on the quality of its management.

Getting back to decision-making, when a decision is taken—one you wouldn't have made yourself—how do you react?

As I have said, I feel that it is enormously important that, through the Corporate Executive Office, the company has the benefit of as much involvement in the decision-making process as possible. I also believe, however, that once a very basic decision is made that that decision should receive the whole-hearted support of everyone in its implementation.

It's like the old saw on foreign policy—differences cease at the water-line. This is not to say that decisions are not scrutinized after the fact if that is what the situation requires. Such scrutiny is, in fact, part of the Corporate Executive Office's responsibility to improve the decision-making process. But broadly speaking, nothing should be done by anyone to undermine the enthusiastic implementation of a decision once it is made.

It is obvious, in the normal course of events, that decisions are made that I would not have made in the same way. Such a situation requires restraint. But basically, I think recognition of the fact that there will be differences of opinion about decisions must preclude any inordinate intrusion on decisions already arrived at.

In other words, there could be more than one right way to do something.

That's right. Different answers don't mean faulty conclusions.

Looking at yourself and at the chief executive officers who preceded you, what do you think are the essential qualities someone who aspires to be in your position should have?

It goes without saying that any candidate for chief executive must have certain basic qualities. In no particular order, I would mention the ability to make sound decisions, a thorough knowledge of the business, a high energy level, a feeling for people, and so forth. I know I am referring to all the usual characteristics one would think of. And having said that, let me add that the qualities and characteristics of an effective chief executive officer can vary from time to time, depending on the circumstances under which a company is functioning—the particular problems, the kinds of priorities, the current challenges it has.

But there are certain basic characteristics, it seems to me, for a chief executive in the life insurance business. First, because of the very nature of our business, he must be an individual of the highest integrity. That is because we involve ourselves, perhaps more deeply than any other business, at the crucial times in the lives of individuals—at the times of death, disability or retirement, or at times of great financial need.

I say integrity, too, because we deal with long-term contracts, agreements which guarantee that the proceeds of the life insurance policy will be paid at a time which can be many years in the future. I also specify integrity because we invest literally billions of dollars to back up these promises to our policyholders.

Second, I think a life insurance chief executive must be someone who has a good feeling for people. We are, after all, a people business. We do not have patents, or natural resources in the ground, or secret processes of some kind. Anyone can manufacture an insurance policy if they've got paper and ink and a press. Therefore, in a very important way, we must have a feeling for people, an understanding of their needs, their aspirations, their problems. That understanding must emanate from a company's top leadership. And I think the chief executive must project this understanding to the public both directly and through the company.

With regard to your policyholders, the responsibility of a life insurance company is rather unique, isn't it? When you talk about "generations of policyholders" it reminds us that Metropolitan assumes obligations that go on for perhaps a hundred years or more.

Yes. We often say that the time when we satisfy many of our contracts will be the time when the people with whom we've contracted are no longer around. That isn't true of most commercial contracts, including our own casualty policies and medical coverage. But with our life insurance policies and pension programs, we're making commitments for many, many years. If someone were to insure his newborn baby with us today, we'd be responsible for payments upon his death for as a long as a century. If the beneficiary of the policy elects to be paid in monthly installments, our obligation could extend even further into the future.

You seem to be saying that in addition to the concern for your policyholders, the public aspects of your job are among your most important responsibilities?

I think that today businessmen generally recognize that an increasing part of their time must be spent dealing with matters that involve the public interest—governmental matters, for example, and a good many matters dealing with corporate social responsibility. This requires, it seems to me, that a company be organized to accommodate these new responsibilities of the chief executive. At Metropolitan we have found that these responsibilities in no way impede the direction or impair the vitality of the company—rather, they enhance it. Other members of the Corporate

Executive Office are able, when necessary, to perform certain company functions that I would ordinarily perform. By the way, the other members of the Corporate Executive Office have similar public interest demands made on them. These new responsibilities require not only the proper allocation of the individual's time, but the correct balance of activity among all of those who make up our Corporate Executive Office.

Do you feel chief executive officers generally are becoming increasingly attentive to what is occurring in the public arena?

Yes, clearly so.

I'd like to talk more about this later on in connection with your work with the City of New York. Just one more question here—do you think that this is now a permanent dimension of the chief executive's job?

Yes. The extent may be variable in future years. But at present we are going through a period of time when the pendulum has swung toward deep involvement in, as you say, the public arena. There may be changes in the ways of handling external activities, but certainly not in the foreseeable future. Today the chief executive must involve himself in matters of the public interest, and in matters particularly dealing with legislation, regulation, and other aspects of government.

There seems to be a feeling—at least a reported feeling—among young people that aspiring to the top spot in an organization carries a price too high to pay. As one who has succeeded to the top, do you agree with that?

I don't agree with it, although my wife probably would. But quite seriously, I think that very few chief executives complain about the pressures of the office. My guess is that most of us really enjoy these pressures and will miss them deeply when the time comes that we no longer have them.

To be sure, unless we are very careful, there is a price paid by our wives and our families. But there are those who have struck a workable balance between family and job exceedingly well. Many others have not. As for myself, I vow each day that I am going to do a better job in this area.

You assumed responsibility at Metropolitan at a time of tremendous change, and there must be times when you are impatient with the performance of people around you, times when your standards aren't met. How does a chief executive cope with this?

I found myself in a unique position when I became chief executive. I assumed the responsibility for implementing changes that I myself had played a part in developing when I was heading up our long-range planning operations.

Since we are undertaking certain changes that no other life insurance company has ever before undertaken, there is no history against which we can compare ourselves. Therefore, there are the ensuing questions, "Is our performance the best we can expect in light of our unprecedented changes?" or "Would it be reasonable to expect even better performance?"

We have had to find our own answers by setting our own year-by-year goals, thus measuring our progress against previous achievements.

So it has been difficult to have standards against which to make evaluations of performance. I suppose this has caused a few of us to have a feeling of uncertainty, but I wouldn't go so far as to call it frustration.

The answer we have found to alleviate this uneasiness lies in trying very hard each year to meet rather specific targets and goals of performance and to use this performance in setting new objectives.

We also compare our performance with what is going on in our industry and with business in general. I think that we are handling our changes extremely well. Our associates seem to understand what it is we are trying to accomplish, and want to be part of it. And I am convinced that the enthusiasm for the changes is continuing to grow among our people.

Could you mention some of the major changes which your company is implementing?

Yes. First, we determined in the sixties that we would no longer be a combination company, selling both debit and Ordinary insurance. We decided to phase out our debit or home collection operation, and become an Ordinary company, concentrating on the sale of larger amount policies, but, of course, providing insurance for all economic groups. It had become evident that the need and demand for the home collection service had decreased greatly. Contributing factors to this steady decrease included greater mobility of the population, the growing number of working wives, the increased use of checking accounts, the rising affluence of policyholders, and the greater insurance coverage being provided through social and group insurance plans.

No other insurance company has attempted anything like this before. So this meant a whole new reorientation of our marketing operation, new recruiting standards, new training procedures, and an expansion of our electronic data processing capability. In short, we embarked on an overall program of raising our standards all the way down the line. The second thing we are doing is realigning our administrative and sales operations under ten head offices and four computer centers across the United States and Canada. Our third decision was to start our own casualty company, which, incidentally, should be operational in most states by 1981. We are in more than twenty states at the present time. Another decision was to have each line of business become self-supporting.

Also, and I think this is particularly important, having made our key decisions, we set out to get more of our people involved in planning, particularly through management by objectives. We want to make sure that everyone in the company knows what role he or she is to play in moving us forward.

Management by objectives is obviously very important to you. How did you grow without it?

We have always had objectives. No question about that. We had our markets and we had our programs for reaching out to those markets. We had a fine marketing organization in place. We were successful, and we had momentum. But as we sensed a more complex market emerging, management by objectives became a more pronounced and identifiable need if we were to achieve our marketing goals.

Now we've been talking about personal insurance marketing. How about group insurance—was there a parallel situation?

No, not in the same sense. There have been dramatic changes in group marketing over the years. For example, we have the capability now of providing coverage to the very smallest of businesses as well as to the very large corporations with tens of thousands of employees. Also, there have been the additions of new coverages, such as dental and vision care, and some very attractive group pension programs which have had remarkable reception by employers in recent years. We've been underwriting group insurance since the beginning—a number of our group customers have been with us for 40 and 50 years—and we're still the largest in the field. But, by and large, the marketing of personal insurance programs for individuals and families is, relatively speaking, more complex.

Okay. Would you say that Metropolitan had some delay in moving into the higher income areas?

The company's greatness was established through the debit business and in urban areas. We had to maintain a presence in those areas in order to service our existing policyholders. Thus, we could not follow the move to the Sun Belt and the suburbs as quickly as we would have liked. Having said this, our most recent moves resulted in our putting our administration and marketing functions closer to these new markets, which, incidentally, has greatly helped us in our ability to develop management.

How?

By opening up jobs that require a wide range of responsibilities. Take our head office in Tampa, which roughly covers an area bordered by Washington, D.C., in the north down to Florida and over to Alabama. The executive who heads that office is running a not-so-small insurance company. My memory is that our Tampa operation alone is larger than all but about thirteen US life insurance companies. In any case, our head office system has provided our management people with a broad range of problem-solving opportunities not possible under the old set-up. On this score alone, the new alignment is invaluable.

Does your revamped management structure allow you to implement changes more rapidly than in the past?

Of course, there has been a period of transition or growing pains, but for the future I'm sure the answer is yes. Interestingly enough, we have to keep an eye on this capability. People often ask me what else we have on the drawing board. Do we want to get into this business or that business? And my theory is that unless we're able to perfect what we're doing now, it would be folly to try to do much else. We're thinking all the time of what we can do differently and better. But at the same time, we've got to be very careful that our reach doesn't exceed our grasp. And I think we understand that.

You know, one of the things you find in business is that it's always easier to get people excited about new projects than to get them involved with solving old problems. But we're faced with some long-term, very basic problems that affect the industry as well. And we've got to motivate people to work on them.

Well, you seem to be going in the right direction. You've begun to change the company more than it has been changed in over a hundred years.

I think it's been very much a cooperative effort. The ideas for change have not all just sprung from any one person. As I said, I was involved in the planning process and so I spent a good deal of time with my associates seeking their views about the company and where it should be headed to benefit our current and future policyholders. I believe we are on the right track and are moving with all deliberate speed.

Okay, you've obviously concentrated on building effective management at Metropolitan. Since you've been so involved with the City of New York, let me ask if you think these management practices would be applicable in government?

No question about it. A governmental body demands the same degree of professional management as a private business. It has the same problems. It has to seek income. It has to attract and train people. It has to build productivity. It has to borrow money. What a business must do to survive, a city must do to survive. And more.

Do you think politicians are only now beginning to realize this?

Well, when I first became involved with New York City and talked about forecasting budgets five years ahead and setting objectives, I was told that you don't do things this way in government. The feeling was that predictions were impossible because so much of the revenue depends on what happens in Washington and at the state level. Planning was almost entirely on a year-to-year basis with little long-range planning at all. Of course, that has all changed and good progress has been made.

Beyond long-range planning, what, specifically, should they be doing?

They must have a system whereby people know they'll be rewarded if they perform better than other people. They must allow a person's leadership ability to be considered on a par with his or her technical or general job knowledge when management appointments are being made. The qualities of leadership should, in fact, be part of every job appraisal. Civil service exams alone are not the best way to identify good managers, even though they are said to have the advantage of being objective.

If government picks managers by another method, how do you prevent manipulation of the process for political purposes?

I think this is an area where the press has a responsibility to be vigilant. They're knowledgeable, and can point fingers at poor appointments. So can business and citizens groups. You know, I think the public is getting restive. They still think there is a lot of room for improvement in the City because their taxes continue to be high and their services are declining. Unfortunately, there's been an abundance of criticism and too few constructive suggestions. There are many dedicated, hardworking civil servants who deserve good leadership at the management level.

The press and public can keep an eye on top appointments, but what about middle management? How do you get the right people into those jobs and make sure they do them well?

By putting people in the upper echelons of management who understand the need to assist in the development of their subordinates and who want them to be more productive. What we need to get away from is not civil service *per se,* but what some people characterize as "the civil service mentality." That mentality does not lead to an environment that motivates people, that recognizes differentials in how well they perform, and that rewards those who perform well. If you had the kind of environment that does those things, I think you'd find that most people want to do a good job, and want to get a sense of satisfaction from what they do. But it won't happen without good management.

Are there other reasons why government hasn't been able to develop management with the same success as business?

In business, if we're doing things right, we spend a lot of time trying to identify people with potential, trying to mold their careers so they can move forward. Career planning is a key activity with us. Individuals find themselves with new assignments, new opportunities, new bosses, but there is a continuity and a stability that makes it possible for them to grow and develop.

That isn't the case in government. When the incumbent mayor of the City of New York loses an election, it signals the fact that it will not be long before there will be new leadership for many of the major departments. A whole new group will come in and most will, in fact, undergo on-the-job training. The civil service people, who stay on through thick and thin, know more about their jobs than the new fellow at the top, and know they will outlast their temporary superiors.

How do you solve that problem?

By making sure that those civil service people are highly trained, that their careers have status and public recognition, that they're well paid. Do you know that only a handful of people in the City's Human Resources Administration make more than $40,000 a year? Yet look at the tremendous responsibility people in that department have. They oversee a four billion dollar a year operation and affect the lives of at least one out of eight people in New York City.

But even if government raises salaries and attracts more qualified civil servants to New York and elsewhere, you'll still have a regularly changing group of politicians at the top. How can you have long-range planning when you've got the political process and the two-year cycle?

It can only happen when the politicians realize that, in the absence of planning, they won't be able to attract or hold business. And unless they can cut administrative costs, they won't ever be able to provide all the services people want. It's a slow process, but I think they're moving in the right direction.

What can business people do to speed up the process?

Well, in the past, I think businessmen too often became involved with government only when it affected them directly. Now they participate more broadly, and they're finding they can influence it more than they thought they could.

When you say, "more broadly," what specifically do you have in mind?

They now accept full-time positions. They are doing this with increasing frequency, because this gives them a chance to have personal, direct impact on government. They also participate in formal advisory groups, as I'm doing in New York, or in informal counseling groups. They encourage internships and work on special studies and research projects. They support political candidates and legislative proposals. They even run for office themselves.

Have you given any thought to running for public office?
No. My wife wouldn't let me.

Can business learn anything from government?
I think so. Government does some things better than we do. They have a better upward-intelligence system, for example. Some even work harder than we do. They also move work more quickly when they want to.

And besides noticing those things, I think a businessman who gets involved with government may gain more compassion for elected officials. After he senses the pressures exerted on them, he might tend to be less critical of the politician personally and more critical of the system at large.

What can government learn from business?

That we're not self-centered. That we're reasonably well-informed. And most importantly, that we needn't always be government's adversary. We'll have differences, but we can work together.

We've proved it in New York City. When we were deeply involved with the governor on "Big MAC" (Municipal Assistance Corporation), we conferred day and night and it was a great experience. He's a Democrat, yet some of his appointees, including myself, were Republicans, but we got along very well, and I think he and his staff knew we'd never mislead them on a problem. The same with the mayor or the first deputy mayor, both of whom I often see for breakfast. We exchange ideas and opinions. We don't always agree, but there's an atmosphere of mutual trust and every report we've written has been published without a word being changed.

You've looked for cooperation, not confrontation?

That's right. I'm impatient with people who operate on the basis of adversary relationships. You know, when I became involved with New York's problems, I found that the press tended to play executives and politicians off against each other. We didn't want the mayor to be reading about our recommendations before he got them from us, so we decided not to talk to the press about committee work. Because our constituency was the mayor and his constituency was the people of New York, we thought it proper that the mayor, and not I, talk to the press, and hence, the people.

What if all your recommendations had been turned down? Would you have gone to the press then?

As I said when I took on the responsibility, I would have resigned if many of our proposals were rejected. Of course, we had not been elected to run the City, but we did feel our suggestions should be given careful, thoughtful and timely study. It has worked just that way. Our pension study, the first in some fifty years, has been fully implemented by legislative actions.

Thanks to that pension study and several others, you've had much more face-to-face experience with union people than most chief executives. I'd be interested to hear some of your general impressions, positive and negative.

The union leaders I've met are well-informed and articulate. They're dedicated to their constituencies, and they believe their job is to improve conditions for their constituents as best they can.

Over the long or short range?

In the past they, too, were mostly short-range oriented, but that has changed. I think they really want to help their people. Above all else they can be trusted—when you talk to them privately, they'll respect the confidence and when they make a commitment, it sticks.

I might add that I think you can deal with union people more effectively when they're secure in their positions. The ones who are threatened at each union election often aren't willing to take a strong stand, so they're harder to work with. They have a tendency to weigh everything not only in terms of substance, but in terms of their own political aspirations. But the secure person knows he can commit the union, and that the members will go along. This is all quite understandable, and is a fact to be considered.

Even with the secure unionists, though, you're in an adversary position.

Yes, but even so we're never enemies. Have you heard the story of the man who's spraying his apple trees? He's really going at it—spraying those trees—and somebody says, "Boy, you must hate bugs." And he says, "No, I just like apples."

In preparing your reports for the City, how closely have you been able to work with the unions?

We have worked with the unions from the first, and there's been great cooperation. While we have not involved them in the beginning on all our studies and reports, we have always kept them very much in mind. I can tell you that we have one study coming up where we plan to ask union people to be part of the task force from the beginning. We're going to go into a large clerical operation and see what can be done to improve productivity.

In the case of our pension study, union experts played a significant role and the reception of the report by almost everyone reflects their important contribution.

Do you keep a close eye on your counterparts at other insurance firms?

Yes, and I've learned a lot from watching them and talking with them. I think we have many very able chief executives in the life insurance business, so I respect them and study their actions carefully. My guess is they're watching us, too.

Well, thank you, Mr. Shinn. You have provided many extraordinary insights into the operation of one of the world's largest corporations, and you have also given us some candid thoughts about the relationships of businessmen with government. Indeed, at times I thought we were talking about a single entity.

In the sense that deliberate thought and planning must go into all human endeavors if they are to be successful, we were talking about the same things.

One final question, then. Is there one statement which would apply to both business and government in relation to what we call success or fulfillment?

I suppose it would be that creative change, managed change, is the key to progress—we must be committed to doing better this year than we did the year before. At Metropolitan, as our people become more involved in the broad issues and problems facing the company, they are beginning to understand this. All of us are realizing that a company like ours is going to be successful in a total way or not successful at all. And I can assure you all of us at Metropolitan are determined to be successful.

Jack K. Busby

*Chairman of the Board and
Chief Executive Officer*
Pennsylvania Power and Light Company

J ack K. Busby, as head of Pennsylvania Power and Light Company, faces constant challenges from regulatory agencies and consumer groups.

But Busby has demonstrated leadership by opening effective dialogues with consumer and environmentalist organizations. He is working aggressively to improve communications with the regulatory agencies as well. In his quarter-century with PP&L, moreover, he has helped to make it one of America's best-managed utilities.

Busby's background is as impressive as the results he has achieved for PP&L. A graduate of Princeton University and Yale University Law School, he has been involved with a diversity of electric industry, community and government groups. He has served as a civilian aide to the Secretary of the Army and as chairman of the Pennsylvania State Planning Board. He has also been a member of the Federal Power Commission's Technical Advisory Committee on Conservation of Energy. And he chaired that commission's National Power Survey Advisory Committee, which reported on reliability standards for electric bulk power supply.

A present director of the Federal Reserve Bank of Philadelphia and of numerous civic, educational, cultural and charitable organizations, he also is active in groups designed to help the electric industry and improve its service to the public. He is on the boards of the National Association of Electric Companies and the Edison Electric Institute (EEI), for example. And he chairs EEI's Energy Anaylsis Division Executive Committee and is an executive committee member of EEI's Environment and Energy Division.

As a utility company, Jack, is PP&L finding it tougher and tougher to do business in this increasingly regulatory climate?

Well, I don't see the kinds of problems we're facing as unique or specially related to the fact that we're a utility company. Over the past ten years, and especially over the past five, a huge umbrella of regulation has been superimposed on almost *all* business activity. So I think the utilities' position as a regulated industry is much less distinctive than it was a few years ago.

If you look at OSHA, EEOC, and all the other social and economic legislation, you find that all businesses have been made into delivery systems for public policy. Take environmental considerations, a very popular and real issue. They're affecting all kinds of businesses. Whether you're in the cement or steel or chemical or paper business or whatever, you're affected directly and heavily.

But you're concerned by the maze of regulation?

Oh, absolutely. Our time and energy are being spent on dealing with too many laws, regulations, and programs which have a wide variety of unconnected purposes and priorities. We find ourselves bogged down in a mishmash of crosscurrents and conflicts.

Let's take the question of pollution. You've spent how much to comply with Environmental Protection Agency regulations?

I don't have the figure right here, but it's been an awful lot of money. First, we've had capital costs. Second, the operating costs of equipment, including the costs of energy needed to run it. Third, we've had direct additional operating expenses over and above the costs of operating, maintaining and paying fixed charges on the equipment.

Such as?

Well, the new regulations affect the nature and therefore the cost of the fuel we burn. They affect the number and necessary qualifications of people we have on the payroll.

Are you managing to keep pace with all these new expenses?

We're still playing catch-up ball, because the costs of yesterday's requirements are still in the process of being incurred and implemented. We've not yet experienced the full impact of environmental regulations and decisions that already exist.

Just the other day, for example, we were looking at our construction-project planning. We're trying to work out a program to meet requirements for plants finished as much as eight or ten years ago. Just to bring them up to today's standards for air quality alone, we visualize spending a minimum of $75 million. That's just the capital investment, and there's a question as to whether we won't have to spend another $75 million beyond it.

The EPA must have the figures, but do they realize what this is costing you in terms of impact on your rates?
I don't think anyone fully realizes it. Not the congressmen, the state legislature, the agencies themselves. Not even people like ourselves who have the requirements directed at us.

Why not?
The difficulty and cost of implementing these regulations are usually learned only after the fact. It's just very difficult to understand how it will work out until we find ourselves in the middle of the playing field. There are too many ripple effects.

Do you think your customers understand what the new regulations have done to their utility bills?
No, absolutely not. I don't think we've done anywhere near a good enough job in communicating with them. We're way behind where we should be.

On the other hand, we have been making progress by working with COCO, the Conference of Consumer Organizations. We first got involved with them when they invited us to participate in a three-day joint conference on utility and energy problems, and we've been in close touch ever since.

Has this relationship been valuable?
It's a conduit for a dialogue with our consumers. And the more we're able to communicate with them, the more we expect of ourselves and the more we understand customer problems and needs. At the same time, the dialogue gives us a chance to inform consumer leaders of our own concerns regarding financial planning, energy conservation, and so on.

Nevertheless, you haven't been able to communicate the correlation between rate hikes and the cost of complying with new regulations?

It's difficult, because the costs are internalized. In other words, the costs of environmental protection and safety and what have you are now being handled through a system that forces producers of goods and services to make investments and increase costs. The expenses are added to the price of those goods and services, but they tend to get lost in the whole inflation problem. It's what Treasury Secretary Blumenthal would call the "infrastructure of inflation," and it's not something that's easily translatable to terms that the public will understand.

In general, how do you think the public views you at present?

Because the businessman is stereotyped as opposing all intervention, controls and the like, people take his statements for granted and discount them. With good reason in this post-Watergate era. The public is particularly suspicious of government and business pronouncements—and unsettled by scientific experts' conflicting assertions.

With regard to energy, therefore, I think the public feels very uncertain and confused. As for higher prices for utilities, it seems they'd prefer to hear that the cause lies with some kind of fraud or with the actions of uncaring managements who are concerned only with making "obscene" profits.

If they did understand the realities, would their attitudes necessarily be different? I'm thinking of your proposal for a "lifeline" rate, which would have exempted from rate increases the first 200 kilowatt-hours of a customer's monthly use. You were trying to satisfy a social need by recognizing the inflation problems of those on low and fixed incomes, and the Public Utilities Commission said "No." I gather what happened was that, when they realized that all other customers would have to pick up the cost of this subsidy, they didn't like it.

That's not quite what happened. That particular proposal got caught up in the middle of a transitional period in public policy. And like many well-intentioned efforts along these lines it failed to satisfy the two wings of the problem. It didn't satisfy the conservative, so-called market-economic user charge philosophy. On the other hand, it didn't go far enough to satisfy those who really wanted to provide substantial protective provisions for the elderly, the low-income people and so on. So it was condemned rather roundly on all sides.

What was your motive in making the proposal?

It was our sense of social responsibility to a considerable degree. We wanted to show that our company was sensitive to the fact that inflation is having an unequal impact on people. A real need for income redistribution has arisen in the country, and we wanted to go on record with the Utilities Commission and the legislative committee as being aware of it. But we admitted that our proposal could be viewed as tokenism, because the problem is so large. We know the solution involves a lot more money and complexity than just monkeying around with a tiny portion of the electric-utility rate.

In your opinion, Jack, how will this issue be resolved in society in general?

It's hard to say, because positions are becoming very polarized. But I think there's still very strong support for a heavy "lifeline" protective provision for a rather substantial volume of use. The so-called subsidized low rate.

Subsidized by whom? Other customers?

Yes, either residential or industrial. And as opinions become polarized as to which group should foot the bill, I think the basic issue that emerges is whether you should use the electric utility rate structure for income redistribution in the first place. Or should you solve the problem through a more sophisticated tool like negative income tax? We endorse the latter view, because we think the problems of having each State Commission apply its own social notions to electric utility rate structures is going to make the whole thing too unpredictable. It's already pretty unpredictable, but that would be chaos.

Did the negative reaction to the "lifeline" proposal surprise you? Did it discourage you? What did you think?

We were a little discouraged, because we thought that some people with whom we'd been working on the basic socioeconomic problem would come forward to support and build on the company's move. But that didn't happen.

The Commission struck down the proposal on the grounds that there wasn't a close enough correlation between the rate adjustment and the customers it was designed to help. There were problems of other users, such as owners of second homes, which suggested that some people might get a free ride. And in retrospect, I think that that was a valid criticism. There really wasn't enough assurance that the benefits would flow to the people who most needed them.

So you weren't upset?
Well, it's always painful to develop what you think is a pretty good program only to learn that it meets neither the wants nor the needs of the consumer. But we've had to go through an evolutionary process in order to identify the consumers' real needs and build mutual trust. I look at the "lifeline" proposal as having been a part of this process.

Okay. We started by talking about regulation, and I'd like to get back to that. There's talk in some industries as to whether the regulators are regulating or are actually getting involved with the problems of management.
In today's world, I don't think regulators can avoid being involved in management.

You see, in past periods of non-inflation, improving technology and service and lower real cost meant that regulators did not have very heavy burdens. They really only had to be there to prevent a total raid on the consumer. The producers of goods and services were doing a better and better job and were, in effect, running contrary to even moderate inflationary tendencies. There was either stability or lower rates or better quality, so real costs were decreasing. And this was true of telephone, gas, electric, everything. So the regulator was in the glorious position of watching over a system that was functioning almost perfectly. In retrospect, I guess we were all coasting on the nice results that were occurring.

And today?
The world has changed in many, many ways. Costs are going up. Income and payment problems are increasing. And people who've been brought up in a system that says you get things done by demonstrating political clout are turning to that—rather than economic solutions—to meet the problems.

Economic factors aren't being fully considered?
Not as much as they should as perceived or respected parts of the solution mechanism. The supply system isn't so popular when prices have to go up. All of a sudden, regulators find themselves right on the front

burner. People are saying to them, "Why aren't you protecting us?" Well, you know, energy and management are complex subjects. And the regulators are coming out of this rather restful period of good results.

Suddenly, they're being asked, "Why are you fellows letting this happen?" Well, when these questions started coming, the first thing an awful lot of regulators had to do was to find out what was happening.

This was in the late sixties?
Yes, and the early seventies. Of course, rates are still going up. We haven't peaked.

Instead of a casual filing for a rate reduction or something like that, in a given case, the regulators have suddenly been deluged by annual applications for increases from everybody and his brother. At the same time, consumer and other groups have been tying rates to social and political causes. And elements which had been taken for granted have abruptly come to the fore.

What kinds of things are you referring to?
The technology of the business, its goals, and the true costs behind it.

So a great turmoil developed in which regulators have had to learn what companies are about, how they function, how they got where they are, where they're trying to go, and whether their objectives make sense from a socioeconomic standpoint. Because all those management decisions ultimately show up in the customers' bills.

So you don't object to the regulators' involvement in management?
No. I think it's necessary today and I welcome it. You know, because of the way rate decisions are made, the regulator is actually *controlling* the management decision-making process. Therefore, regulators and their staffs must be as competent as the utility managers themselves. Otherwise, we all are running the risk of a hell of an accident.

What about the regulators' staffs, Jack? How competent are they?
In too many cases they're overworked, underpaid, and lacking the additional people and new blood necessary to handle this hurricane.

In order to attract good people, you know, the regulatory agencies have to have a record of professionalism, and of effectively solving tough problems. A good MBA would love to a get a few years experience in a well-run regulatory commission. But if he doesn't perceive it as being professionally run and thinks he'll be used as just a pair of hands, you're going to have trouble attracting him.

Could you give me an example of the sort of management problems that a regulatory agency might today have to get involved in?

Well, one perfectly appropriate part of regulation is to control conditions under which a customer might be disconnected for nonpayment of a bill. Related to that is regulation of the terms of credit. For example, if you don't pay your bill on time, how long should we wait before we disconnect? If you are disconnected, what charges must you pay to have service restored? What about security deposits? If you're overdue on a bill, how much should we charge to motivate you to pay your bill on time? All of these questions are logical areas for regulation.

Now, as a result of the severe winter of 1976–1977, many commissions have found it appropriate to direct utilities like us not to disconnect anyone. They've also involved themselves in the questions of what kinds of credit terms we should grant. Well, at some point, if customers learn that they won't be disconnected whether or not they pay, we'll be in the retail-financing business up to our eyeballs.

So the regulators have really made a major management decision?

Right. Here is a proper area of regulation. And yet its impact on our cash-flow can be vast. Because our cash-flow is designed to build facilities, not for retail credit.

You mentioned that the commissioners have also set interest rates for unpaid bills?

The Commission has proposed an interest-rate system with a charge of only one-half of one per cent per month. Our financial officer looked at this and said facetiously, "Well, that's good news. I know how to play this game. I won't pay my bill!" Anyone who knows the borrowing rate in the marketplace will say that our penalty runs almost neck and neck with borrowing from your insurance company.

So this situation exemplifies, I think, how problems can develop. The commissioners need to respond to human and social needs. But at the same time, they need to have managerial and financial sophistication. Otherwise, their decision-making will be unbalanced and will inadvertently produce wrecks.

When the regulators decided about nonpayment and penalties, do you think they realized what they were going to do to your cash-flow?

I doubt very much whether that factor was considered, which illustrates why I believe we've got a long way to go on the learning curve. You know, I sound like Johnny One-Note. But I don't see how we can have effective regulation without sophisticated regulators. Because unless they understand the interactions and ripple effects and practice a really in-depth systems-management approach to regulation, there's going to be a series of knee-jerk reactions which will just pyramid the problems. And when that happens, ironically, people say, "Well, that just proves the market economy doesn't work. We'd better scrap the whole system and start over."

They make the problem, and then they cite it as proof that you can't act effectively.

It certainly looks that way sometimes, but I must emphasize my belief that it's part of the business world's responsibility to help people understand why decisions are made as they are. We've got to discuss them openly as opposed to just saying, "This is the way it is." We have to explain choices and say, "These are the consequences of going this route and these are the consequences of going that route. Now, doesn't it make sense to go this way?" You know, we can sit in our closets and complain, or we can go out there and patiently, unendingly work to cultivate understanding from the public.

But what about the commissioners? How can you educate them in the present climate?

It used to be easy, because it wasn't considered immoral for people to sit around a table to discuss problems, explore alternatives and develop understandings. But today, regulators are under new pressure to be aloof. We often now exchange views only in adversary proceedings.

There's virtually no informal contact?

That's right. Contact either way in many instances is now officially prohibited whenever we have a formal proceeding before them. And for our own protection, we define "proceeding" broadly to include not only our rate cases, but many industry-related issues they may be considering.

So the limitation of discussion is very real. And I think it's a reflection of this Watergate recovery period we're going through. We want people to work together and yet we set up criteria which require an almost monastic isolation.

You're obviously unhappy with the trend.
I'm not saying it's all bad, but it doesn't make communications any easier. I think, ultimately, we're just going to have to recognize that we're losing more than we're gaining by artificial constraints in the name of purity. Meanwhile, we can try to work around the situation. We can no longer talk directly, so new forums are being created to fill the gap.

What sorts of new forums?
After feeling some of the same pressures as the regulators, for example, some of the people in our state legislature began to develop a more-than-passing, expedient interest in energy questions. So they started to look at them in depth. And they created a mechanism in this state for formal and informal hearings which are open to the public and which involve utility people and commissioners as well as members of the legislature. The Consumer Advocate attends to represent consumers officially.
I hope it won't turn out to be a process where utility people complain to legislators and legislators jump on commissioners. That won't solve anything. The point should be to get at issues. You know, what are the needs? Are they legitimate? How can we meet them? We've got to address those questions and we've got to professionalize the communications process.

So far, do the hearings look like a step in that direction?
They're an awful lot better than nothing. And I'm hopeful that we can all remain patient and keep in mind that we're trying to learn how to work with one another.

Do you personally take part in the hearings?
Yes, but we're also trying to involve other people in the company, because the problem is so large that no one person could ever cover it. We have to multiply our communications impact, and that means educating people within our own company.

What attitude do the commissioners take toward the legislative hearings?
I think they welcome them, because they get a chance to have dis-

cussions that they really want to have. They perceive problems and discomfort. And I think they wonder every now and then what's going on. Yet they can't pick up the phone, call someone in a utility, and have lunch or something.

Do all the regulators attend the hearings?
Some do and some don't. But I think the ones who do are learning. Now, whether they're learning as quickly and as qualitatively as we'd like is open to discussion. But I certainly see a recognition that the responsibilities and difficulties of regulation are on a par with those of management.

Are they gaining more sophistication in financial areas? For example, when you build a new generating plant, as I understand it, the commissioners won't allow you to charge a penny of the cost to your customers until the facility is completed and in service.
What you say is exactly true, but there's another side to the story. Because, in calculating the rate of return they'll allow, the commissioners consider the cost of money. In other words, property under construction isn't included in rate-base but the regulators do take into account what it's costing us to raise money to build these new facilities.

You're saying they'll allow a rate of return that reflects what you're currently paying for money. But you can't get that return on money you raise for a new plant until that plant is finished.
That's right. And it really doesn't make as much difference as we might think whether construction work in progress is in the rate-base or not. The bottom line is, what are your earnings? Their quality? What are your interest coverages and dividends? What is the relationship between market price and book value? How good is the cash flow in relation to construction needs? What's the quality of your securities? These are some of the key bottom-line figures.
So one doesn't want to get drowned in a particular methodology. Because there are many ways to regulate that will tell the investor that regulators are sensitive to bond ratings, interest coverage, dividends, book value, market price, and so on.

But are the regulators really sensitive to these figures? You've had great operating results over the past ten years; yet your stock is selling at roughly one-third of what it was a decade ago. You've had to retain more and more of your earnings for reinvestment, so there's been a declining return to the shareholders. Isn't this an indictment of the way the regulatory process has worked?

The common-stock owner in utilities today finds himself in a much higher-risk business than was conceived of some time ago. And the rate of return is no longer commensurate with the risk. That's why, I believe, there's a revolution of expectations and analysis going on in this area.

You know, investment analysts used to rate only companies. Well, now they're rating Utility Commissions, because they perceive that that's where the action is. They know that if a Commission is hell-bent on decapitating the utilities it's regulating, genius within a utility isn't going to help it any more than it helped Sir Thomas More.

Well, the Commissions have felt pretty comfortable in making your shareholders bear the burdens rather than the customers. Isn't that what it's amounted to?

The shareholders have taken on an undue burden. And I think the issue is whether the Commissions are facing up to the fact that, unless rates are sufficient to attract capital, the customer will not be served over the long term.

If utilities remains a low-return, high-risk industry, in other words, you won't be able to get the capital that you need to do a good job for the customer.

That's right. We're projecting a capital investment of about two billion dollars in the next five years, and about two-thirds of that will have to come from the outside. Because of the way regulation and cash-flow work, there's no way we can raise it unless the regulatory people take an approach that is less expedient and more reassuring to the investor.

You know, we try not to be alarmists about this, but we're at a point where we've got to give the investor some reasonable basis for hope for the future. We don't have to be a Polaroid, a Xerox, or an IBM, but the investor does have to know that he won't be cannibalized.

As, to some degree, he has been.

Well, I think everyone understands that you can have good periods and bad periods. And one way of looking at it is to say that the sixties was a very good period for utilities and the seventies aren't so good.

Now, maybe some people in the sixties thought that that was the norm and that it would go on forever. That's a delusion. By the same token, I don't think the present situation will exist forever. It's an adjustment period.

I think the average investor understands that and has not lost confidence in the utility industry. But he's sensitive to signals, like the fact that his dividends have fallen way behind increases in the Consumer Price Index. And he's looking at things more cynically and analytically, wondering whether he's going to be given a fair shake.

You've seen those *Wall Street Journal* ads where companies point out what the Consumer Price Index has done in recent years and how that index is related to stock value and dividends. Well, every time that kind of ad appears, it puts pressure on the equity/capital-raising prospects of the utilities. Because people are naturally going to become more sophisticated, they're not going to put their money on slow horses if fast ones are available. That's economic reality.

Okay, now what about political reality? In Pennsylvania, representatives serve two years and senators have four-year terms. When you talk, say, about a coal-generating plant that will be completed in thirteen years, do they really care?

Well, this is where you get down to the gut issue of whether you're an optimist or not.

And you're an optimist?

I've got to be. If I'm not, I ought to get out and let somebody who is an optimist take charge.

You know, if you look back over this country's history, you'll see a whole lot of optimists who made commitments and took huge risks based on their conceptions of the future. Optimism may have been out of style recently, but I see signs now of people in public life working much harder to make the system work and deal with the future. They're trying to work around the short-term political pressures to achieve sensible long-term results.

Still, if a politician is up for re-election and can gain votes by championing the consumer who suffers from high electric bills, isn't it a big temptation for him to go after you?

I think it is. But I think there are two lifesavers in that situation. One, there's competition for public office. And two, people aren't stupid.

No, they're intelligent. But they're not informed about the complexities of your business.

But they're sophisticated in that they understand that there's no free lunch. When someone promises that these days, they know they're getting a bag of promises rather than any real prospects of a sandwich.

Consequently, I see signs now of people being elected who say we have to face issues and make tough decisions. The people who offer quick solutions are in many cases going to the sidelines. It's no longer easy to just lead people down a garden path.

Even assuming that politicians are beginning to face up to reality, you've still got a maze of bureaucracy to deal with. When you tried to build a pipeline recently, you mentioned well over a dozen regulatory agencies that had to approve the project. And approval was so slow in coming that you wound up spending a lot of money for things that ultimately were not required.

That's right. The project took only six months for construction, but we spent three years getting all the necessary clearances. As a result of the delays, it became necessary for us to construct a $2.3 million alternate rail-unloading facility to assure that we could get sufficient fuel. Our customers had to foot the bill.

What have the regulators subsequently said about this?

So far, at least, the investment has not been denigrated. But the ballgame is still under way. One hopes that the commissioners as well as the legislators won't simply say, "Gee, that was a bad decision." A better approach would be for them to say, "What were the conditions that existed at the time of the decision? What went wrong that we can learn from? What can we do to avoid these kinds of management decision-making dilemmas, delays and frustrations in the future?" And, hopefully, the Commission will be looking at its own decision-making in terms of these same dilemmas, which they're faced with whether or not they like to think so.

You'd like to see a learning process emerge from this?

Sure. You know, one has to look at accidents from the standpoint of preventing future ones, rather than from the standpoint of hanging somebody. The latter is the first reaction, of course, because it's easier to find fault than it is to solve problems. But we've got to keep struggling.

On your pipeline, why did approval take so long?

It wasn't really the regulators' fault. What held it up was that some people felt this was environmentally inappropriate. And under a free society, they had a right to seek protection of their interests through court litigation. They invoked certain environmental-protection laws and regulations which produced substantial litigation and caused the delay.

But you finally won?

Yes, the pipeline is operating. And it saved our necks last winter. Without it, we never would've been able to get all the fuel we needed.

Do you think the environmentalists who opposed you ever considered that possibility? Are they now saying to themselves, "Gee, we want to protect the environment but, if we'd won the pipeline battle, there might have been supply problems and people out of work last winter"? Or don't they think that way?

Well, there are always extremists who say, "I don't care about that. It's somebody else's problem. This is my way and that's it." So there has to be more flexibility, more appraisal of individual issues. And less one-shot decision-making.

You know, there's a case now where the TVA, with Congress' authority, was building a dam in Tennessee. Well, it turned out that the dam was going to wash out a stretch of river where a little fish called the "snail darter" has its home. This eight-mile stretch is the only place in the US where the snail darter lives. And since it's on the endangered species list, a judge has now forced TVA to bring its whole project to a halt. It's a case of good intentions but no understanding of the implications.

In the case you're talking about, one environmentalist was quoted as saying that "you have to draw the line somewhere and those fish are important." How do you persuade someone like that?

Well, he may be right and he may be wrong. The point is that we need more zones of decision-making and fewer of these immutable lines. It always seems like life is simpler if you have a line instead of a zone. But there has to be room for give and take. The single-shot ruling, the firm line of demarcation, creates more problems than it solves.

You know, it's self-defeating to assert values to the point where it becomes impossible for the system to function. And I believe that a large number of environmentalists are adjusting to that reality. We're beginning to talk with them about ways to have regard for values and still have the system function.

You've opened a dialogue?

Yes. We've set up a permanent advisory task force to discuss sites for future power plants. And we're putting all our cards on the table and getting a lot of people involved. We haven't selected a bunch of patsies. We've told people that if, as we go down the road, they think others should be brought into the process, it's fine with us.

This sounds like the sort of open exchange you can no longer have with the regulators.

Exactly. Instead of people comfortably enjoying their polarized views and shooting at one another, these people are saying that there's room for compromise. And they don't feel permanently contaminated or disgraced just because they have lunch with a utility manager. They're saying, "Maybe they're acting in good faith and, as long as I feel that way, we ought to keep talking."

Holding dialogues with environmentalists and other public-interest groups requires a whole new style of management, doesn't it?

Well, the need for change was easy to see. In the old days when we wanted to get from point A to point B, we got out our mental ruler and saw right away where we needed to build lines. This won't wash anymore. We have to say we have made changes not out of a sense of nobility or virtue, but in the interests of survival.

You have good contacts with the management people in other utilities around the country. What do you think has been the psychological impact on them of this whole change in style that the times have mandated?

It's probably the best thing that's ever happened to the psychiatric profession.

You know, it's very, very hard to have committed yourself to economic efficiency and to have achieved high competence in that area and to then suddenly have economic efficiency by only one of many loosely-defined elements. It's also difficult to be involved in conflicts and decision-making for which one wasn't trained and to which one has had no exposure. It just descends upon one, and it's very wearing.

In making decisions, you can't consider just economics anymore. You have to weigh social factors as well.

I think so. We still need to provide economical, reliable service to the customers, but it's now just as important that we do so in an open, responsive and responsible way.

Jack K. Busby

I'm not saying that we should make decisions to be popular. But we can't accomplish reconciliation through a we-know-best attitude or a strictly political mandate. To really legitimize our decisions, they have to be such that independent third parties would consider them well-made, tough-minded, and effective. The public assumption is that an awful lot of business decisions are not legitimate in that sense. To overcome this feeling by making the public more aware of our decision-making process is what I mean by being open, responsive, and responsible.

And you feel that some utility managers have had trouble adjusting to this challenge?

When we consider that we've been in the "new world" only about four or five years now, the degree of adjustment and acceptance seems rather remarkable. Many utility managers have set broader, less definite objectives while maintaining their sense of values.

There are some people who've just thrown in the towel, either officially or internally. What's remarkable, though, is the number of people who haven't. Their commitments to themselves and to effective performance have carried them through an awful lot of change.

Will the next generation of utility managers adjust more easily?

Nobody knows. They might well be better, more alert, and more knowledgeable as a result of what we've been through. Or they might be sloppier and more prone to say, "It's so complex, so impossible, and so many conflicting objectives are being imposed that to hell with it." But I'm hopeful, because the people coming up today are better prepared than we were. They're better people-managers and better systems-managers, because they're more professionally trained to understand the dynamics of problem-solving.

You know, one must bring to problems not only a desire for reconciliation but also a sense of direction around which you look for solutions. One can always buy accommodation for a price and, in a sense, resolve a conflict. But peace at any price will ultimately buy some very nasty long-term problems. So there has to be a sense of direction, a central theme, behind problem-solving. And that makes it very tough.

Especially since the problems themselves are getting tougher.

Yes. We're in the same turmoil that conventional industrial and commercial firms are now facing. And then as a bonus, we have to deal with the current turmoil in the energy field and with all sorts of other new problems.

For example, investment decisions have always been important, but they weren't anywhere near as critical as they are now. In the middle or early sixties, I don't think anyone stayed awake at night worrying whether plant construction might suddenly come to a halt because of an EPA order or whatever. So there are very different kinds of investment risks today than there were yesterday. The situation is much more sophisticated and involves whole new evaluations of one's responsibilities for raising capital.

If you had a chance to say one thing to your fellow chief executives, what would it be?

Hang in there with a sense of humor as long as you feel you're effective. But realize that, at some point, the wear and tear can make your efforts counterproductive. And when that point comes, it's a good sign that you ought to look around for somebody whose nerve ends are in better shape. Because we need people who are ready to go at full throttle. Anybody who's not shouldn't have his hand on the tiller.

About the Author

Chester Burger has served as management consultant to more than 225 major U.S. corporations. President of Chester Burger & Co., Inc., of Madison Avenue, New York since 1964, he was formerly President of Communications Counselors, Inc., and earlier, was National Manager of CBS Television News.

Since 1955 he has been a consultant to American Telephone and Telegraph Company. Over the years he has served as a guest lecturer at such schools as The University of Michigan Graduate School of Business Administration, the New School for Social Research, and Dalhousie University.

Mr. Burger is the author of *Survival in the Executive Jungle, Executives Under Fire, Executive Etiquette,* and *Walking the Executive Plank.*

He is a member and a former director of the Public Relations Society of America, a former trustee and Secretary of the National Urban League, and an Honorary Member of Telephone Pioneers of America. Mr. Burger is listed in "Who's Who in America."